DEEPLY ROOTED IN NORTH CAROLINA

Two Runaway Slave Brothers Forever Separated After Joining the Union Army

"Spirit of Freedom"

A 154-YEAR-OLD MYSTERY SOLVED

Dr. Juanita Patience Moss

Foreword by Dr. Frank Smith, Founding Director
African American Civil War Museum

HERITAGE BOOKS
2019

HERITAGE BOOKS
AN IMPRINT OF HERITAGE BOOKS, INC.

Books, CDs, and more—Worldwide

For our listing of thousands of titles see our website
at
www.HeritageBooks.com

Published 2019 by
HERITAGE BOOKS, INC.
Publishing Division
5810 Ruatan Street
Berwyn Heights, Md. 20740

Copyright © 2019 Dr. Juanita Patience Moss

Heritge Books by the author:
Anthracite Coal Art of Charles Edgar Patience
Battle of Plymouth, North Carolina (April 17–20, 1864): The Last Confederate Victory
Created to Be Free: A Historical Novel about One American Family
Deeply Rooted in North Carolina: Two Runaway Slave Brothers Forever Separated After Joining the Union Army
The Forgotten Black Soldiers in White Regiments During the Civil War, Revised Edition
Tell Me Why Dear Bennett: Memoirs of Bennett College Belles, Volumes I-III

Cover art by artist Joel Ulmer
Inspired by re-enactor Michael Hinton
Photo by Reba N. Burruss-Barnes, publicist

All rights reserved. No part of this book may be reproduced or transmitted in any form or by any means, electronic or mechanical, including photocopying, recording or by any information storage and retrieval system without written permission from the author, except for the inclusion of brief quotations in a review.

International Standard Book Number
Paperbound: 978-0-7884-5871-2

This book is dedicated
to

Pvt. Crowder Patience
103rd PA Volunteers
Company C
&
Pvt. Thomas Patience
5th MA Colored Cavalry
Company B

"Once let the black man get upon his person the brass letters 'U.S.,' let him get an eagle on his button, and a musket on his shoulder and bullets in his pocket, and there is no power on earth which can deny that he has earned the right to citizenship in the United States."

Frederick Douglass

...AND TO THE FIRST GRIOT[1] OF THE PATIENCE FAMILY

**Fourth Child of
Crowder and Elsie Veden Patience**

Lillian Maria Patience Cuff

(1883-1986)

The 1924 Graduate

The Practical Bible Training School
Binghamton, N.Y.

(author's collection)

CONTENTS

FOREWORD		vii
PREFACE		ix
PHOTOGRAPHS AND DOCUMENTS		x
INTRODUCTION		13
ACKNOWLEDGEMENTS		15
Chapter 1	The Pennsylvania Patiences	17
Chapter 2	What's in a name?	21
Chapter 3	Pvt. Crowder Pacien the soldier	23
Chapter 4	Crowder Patience the citizen	37
Chapter 5	Learning about Black soldiers in the Civil War	57
Chapter 6	Pvt. Thomas Patience's name on the Wall of Honor	61
Chapter 7	Pvt. Thomas Patience the soldier	67
Chapter 8	Confusing surname spellings	83
Chapter 9	The brother who returned Home	85
Chapter 10	Thomas Patience the citizen	87
Chapter 11	Pension applications and affidavits	93
Chapter 12	Revelations found on pension Applications	103
Chapter 13	Thomas Patience's pension increases	107
Chapter 14	Valuable clue from North Carolina	119
Chapter 15	The 154-year-old mystery is solved	125
Chapter 16	Concluding evidence	129
Chapter 17	Questions still unanswered	135
Chapter 18	*In Memoriam*	137
Appendix I	Tracing the Patience Y-Chromosome	141
Appendix II	First generations of Pennsylvania Patiences	142

Appendix III	Paternal pedigree of Matthew Allen Patience	143
Appendix IV	Pedigree of Joseph R. Lawrence Jr.	145
Appendix V	Francois Briols and nine slaves	146
Appendix VI	Petition granted to Francois Briols	147
Appendix VII	Formation of United States Colored Troops	149
Appendix VIII	General Orders No. 323	150
NOTES		151
SOURCES		165
TESTIMONIALS		177

OH, FREEDOM

"Oh, Freedom, Oh, Freedom,

Oh, Freedom over me.

And before I'll be a slave,

I'll be buried in the grave

And go home to my Lord and be free."

Negro Spiritual

FOREWORD

by
Dr. Frank Smith, Founding Director
African American Civil War Memorial Museum

Dr. Juanita Patience Moss is charismatic, professional and determined. In the search to find more of her own family history, she has written *Deeply Rooted in North Carolina* in which she has solved the mystery of two formerly enslaved brothers motivated by the quest for freedom becoming lost and separated from each other for 145 years following the Civil War. The story of Thomas Patience and Crowder Patience as told by descendant Juanita Patience Moss will inspire everyone to start digging for your family story.

Dr. Moss is a frequent visitor at the African American Civil War Memorial and Museum where she has shared her research about freedom seeking blacks who joined regular Union Army regiments in the Civil

War. Their names were not enrolled in the Bureau of US Colored Troops file at the National Archives and therefore are not engraved on the monument in Washington, D. C. One such soldier was her great grandfather, Pvt. Crowder Patience, who served with the 103rd Pennsylvania Volunteers.

She has done her family and the world a great service by delving into the thousands of Union Civil War records to confirm thousands of lost names of blacks who served in regular Union regiments before the Emancipation Proclamation declared free all enslaved blacks and allowed them to enlist in the Union Army.

In her book, *Deeply Rooted in North Carolina*, Dr. Moss relates how, due to her unyielding desire to discover her freedom fighting family history, she found a great-great uncle, Pvt. Thomas Patience, who had been a member of the 5th MA Colored Cavalry. He is listed among the 209,145 names on the Wall of Honor of the African American Civil War Memorial in Washington, D. C.

These names are engraved on stainless steel plaques in alphabetical order in regiments and they fly off the Wall when a descendant such as Juanita Patience Moss shows up and tells us the family story. The book is a tribute to her research and hard work and we are lucky to be able to share the story of her family journey to freedom and liberation.

PREFACE

This book documents how a mystery begun in 1864 was solved in 2018. It is a mystery that commenced during the Civil War and concluded when *23andMe*[2] connected Edenton, North Carolina, cousins.

The mystery concerns two tenacious young slaves absconding from bondage and then enlisting in the Union Army, both under the surname "Patience." Thomas Patience joined the 5th MA Colored [Col'd] Cavalry and Crowder Patience, the 103rd PA Volunteers.

After the Union victory, Thomas would return home to Edenton where he remained until his death in December 1929. Crowder would travel with his regiment to Harrisburg, Pennsylvania, to receive his last pay. He would remain in that state until his death in January 1930. Descendants have wondered if the two are brothers, and that question has finally been answered.

Solved, also, is a second mystery. Why does Pvt. Thomas Patience, with name inscribed on the Wall of Honor[3] surrounding the bronze monument "Spirit of Freedom"[4] in Washington, D.C., not have a Union tombstone in Chowan County, North Carolina, where he is buried?[5] On the other hand, why is Pvt. Crowder Patience's name not inscribed on the Wall of Honor in Washington, D.C., even though a Union tombstone marks his gravesite in a cemetery in West Pittston, Pennsylvania?

Dr. Juanita Patience Moss

Alexandria, Virginia
December 31, 2018

PHOTOGRAPHS & DOCUMENTS

The 1924 Graduate	iv
Dr. Frank Smith	vii
Newly Found Cousins Meet for the First Time	xii
Lillian Maria Patience Cuff	18
Four Generations Celebrate Aunt Lillie's 98th Birthday	20
Aunt Lillie's 100th Birthday Party	20

CROWDER PATIENCE'S STORY

Pvt. Crowder Patience's Union Tombstone	21
Map of the Albemarle Sound	23
Pvt. Crowder Pacien's Enlistment Record	24
Pvt. Croder Pacien in Co. C Descriptive Book	25
Pvt. Crowder Pacien's Co. Muster Roll for Jan. & Feb. 1864	26
"Siege of Plymouth, N C" Historic Marker	28
Pvt. Crowder Pacien Co. C Muster Roll for Mar. &Apr. 1864	30
Pvt. Crowder Pacien Detached to Roanoke Island	31
Pvt. Crowder Pacien's Muster-Out	33
Pvt. Crowder Pacien's Discharge Certificate	34-35
Keystone State Anthracite Coal Plaque	36
Crowder Patience Standing Soldier-Straight at Age 81	37
Patience Business Card	39
Veteran Crowder Patient's Invalid Pension Increase	41
Crowder Patience With G.A.R. Comrades	42
Compilation of Crowder Patience, Discharge & Flag	49
Crowder Patience's Death Certificate	50
Application for Military Headstone	53
Crowder Patience's Tombstone Next to Wife Elsie's	54
Widow's Pension for Elsie Veden Pacient	55
National Civil War Museum Brick Commemoration	56

THOMAS PATIENCE'S STORY

"Spirit of Freedom" Monument	57
Pvt. Thomas Patience's Inscribed Name	61
Pvt. Thomas Patience's Name Enlarged	62

Pvt. Thomas Patience Was Born in Chowan County, N.C.	63
Providence African American Cemetery	65
Warren Grove Baptist Church	65
Pvt. Thomas D. Patience's Volunteer Enlistment	67-68
Pvt. Thomas D. Patience's Recruit Declaration	69
Pvt. Thomas D. Patience's Muster and Description Roll	70-71
Pvt. Thomas Patience's Co. Muster Roll - May & June 1864	72
Pvt. Thomas Patience's Co. Muster Roll - Sept. & Oct. 1864	73
Pvt. Thomas Patience's Co. Muster Roll - Nov. & Dec. 1864	75
Pvt. Thomas Patience's Co. Muster Roll - Mar. & April 1865	76
Pvt. Thomas Patience's Co. Muster Roll - May & June 1865	77
Pvt. Thomas Patience on Co. B Returns July 1865	78
Pvt. Thomas Patience's Muster-out Roll	79
Youngest Presenter Matthew Allen Patience with Family	81
Matthew Patience -Youngest Descendent Presenter	82
Surname Spelled Pashons/Patience	83-84
W. W. Harris Witnessed Thomas Patience's Return Home	87-88
Pension Application	90
Thos Pashion's First Invalid Pension Application	94
Major Bonn and John R. Davis' Affidavits	97-98
Thomas Patience's Declaration For Pension in 1907	100-101
W. W. Harris Witnessed Thomas Patience's Mark	102
Chowan County Courthouse	106
Thomas Patience's First Pension Payment	107-108
John Standing's Affidavit for Thomas Patience's Identity	109-110
Thomas Patience's Pension Increase in 1910	111-112
Thomas Patience's Request to Commissioner of Pensions	113
Lawyer's Letter to Commissioner of Pensions	114
Thomas Patience's Pension Increase to $24.00 Per Month	115
Thomas Patience's Declaration for Pension Increase	116-117
Thomas Patience's Drop Report in 1929	118
Thomas Patience's Death Certificate	119
Answers to Questions Pertaining to a Wife	123
Four Generations of Edenton Lawrences	124
Pvt. Thomas Patience's Inscribed Name on the Wall	128
Thomas Lawrence's Receipt	131
Thomas Patience's Chattel Mortgage Receipt	131
A Chattel Mortgage for Thomas Patience in 1910	132

The Chattel Mortgage Marked Paid	133-134
Joseph Lawrence Jr. Finds His Ancestor's Name on the Wall	137
Lawrence Family	137
Thomas Patience's Certificate of Honor from	138
Two Civil War Brothers	139
Lawrence Siblings Joseph and Connie	145
African American Civil War Entrance Gate	164
Sankofa	176
Michael Hinton, Re-enactor 23rd USCT	177

<u>*Newly Found Cousins Meet for the First Time*</u>
Juanita Patience Moss and Joseph Lawrence Jr.
(photo by Reba N. Burruss-Barnes, Publicist)
May 30, 2018

INTRODUCTION

Some readers may be curious about how I happened to become the griot for the Patience clan. "Why you, Juanita, and not one of your relatives?"

The answer is that I had the most exposure to the Patiences because after my parents' divorce, I was reared by my great grandmother, Elsie Veden Patience (widow of my great grandfather, Crowder) and two of their daughters, Jessie and Lillian. By living in their home, I would become acquainted with four generations of Patiences and was exposed to bits and pieces of family lore that intrigued me. Most of what I know came from Lillian Maria (pronounced Maw-rye-ah) Patience Cuff, whose longevity to almost her 103rd birthday in 1986 provided many years for plying her with questions.

Because the Patience surname is so unique, my family has speculated that perhaps our slave ancestor, like many other fugitives, may have chosen that name to elude capture by his master. Since Crowder could not spell it, his surname has been recorded with different spellings: "Pacien," "Pashons," "Pacient," and "Patient."

According to Aunt Lillie, when Crowder and Elsie's first child Florence, entered the first grade in West Pittston, Pennsylvania, her teacher recorded her surname as "Patience." Since then for at least nine generations, our family has been known by that name, but not until 2018 would we discover who we really are.

We have discovered that we Pennsylvania Patiences are a branch of a proud North Carolina family—albeit known by a different surname.

My first book, *Created to Be Free,* published in 2001 is a historical novel based on the lives of my great grandparents, Crowder and Elsie Veden Patience. I could not write their biographies because I did not know enough about them. Why had I felt such an urgency to write about those secretive great grandparents, anyway? I write for later generations who sometime in the future might want to learn about them.

Much of what I wrote in *Created to Be Free* is historical fiction containing my imaginings of what could have transpired in many known situations. For my relatives, I included a list of facts to help separate truth from fiction. By weaving facts with fiction, my goal was to relate how former slaves and their freeborn children had to strive to survive during the post-Civil War era.

My research began in 1998. Twenty years later, I have written this nonfiction sequel to share some of what I have learned since publishing *Created to Be Free*. For instance, through *Ancesty.com* DNA testing, our first male Patience ancestor has been traced generations back to Cameroon.[6] Also, through *23andMe* DNA testing, we Pennsylvania Patiences have been introduced to heretofore unknown relatives also deeply rooted in North Carolina.

ACKNOWLEDGEMENTS

In Memoriam

2nd -Cousin Florence Patience Glover Smith
Artist- Joseph Mills
Curator- Hari Jones, African American Civil War Museum
Curator- Harry Thompson, Port 'O Plymouth Museum
Father- C. Edgar Patience, Anthracite Coal Sculptor
Great Aunt- Lillian Maria Patience Cuff
Historian- Glenda McWhirter Todd, 1st AL U.S. Cavalry
Historian- William Gladstone
Husband- Edward Irving Moss
Uncle- Robert Jesse Patience

Many thanks to:

1st Cousin- Christine Patterson
1st Cousin- Katherine Patience Kennedy
2nd Cousin- Anthony Patience
2nd Cousin- Jason Patience
3rd Cousin- Connie Lawrence
3rd Cousin- Joseph R. Lawrence Jr.
3rd Cousin- LeRoy Crowder Patience Jr.
3rd Cousin- Matthew Allen Patience
4th Cousin- Cynthia Lawrence
4th Cousin- Tanya Lawrence
Artist- Joel Ulmer
Curator- Joanne Hyppolite Ph.D., National Museum of African American History and Culture, Washington, D.C.
Curator- Earl L. Ijames, North Carolina Museum of History, Raleigh, N.C.
Daughter- Brenda Moss Green, Esq.
Edenton Town Manager- Anne-Marie Knight

Family Genealogist- Regina Lawrence
Founding Director-Frank Smith Ed.D, African American Civil War Museum, Washington, D.C.
Friend- Brenda Morgan Nicholson
Friend & Editor- Cheryl Chevalier Ph.D.
Friend- Robert Nardone
Friend & Editor- Ruth Baskerville Ph.D.
God-daughter- Nikki Johnson
Great Nephew- Ryan Patience
Great niece- Suzanne von Briesen Wagner
Historian- Bennie McCrae
Historian- Danny Lehan
Librarian- Rosalie Boyd Miller
Niece- Diana Patience Medieros
Niece- Heidi Patience von Briesen
Niece- Teresa Patience Ojeda
Photographer- Philip Dente
Publicist- Reba Nadine Burruss-Barnes, REBASSOCIATES
Publisher- Craig Scott, C.E.O. of Heritage Books, Inc.
Raleigh Civil War Roundtable Member- Robert Farrell
Re-enactor- Michael Hinton, 29th USCT
Reporter- Jack Smiles
Son- Eric Douglas Moss
Visionaries & Friends- Earl &Mary Brown

And to the myriad more who have offered encouragement.

THE PENNSYLVANIA PATIENCES

Until very recently, my paternal family has known no ancestors other than Crowder and Elsie Veden Patience. We did know, however, that our patriarch had shared with his children the fact that he had been a runaway slave who had escaped from an "Edington," N.C., plantation before becoming a soldier in the Union Army. Many years after his death, I would discover he had mispronounced "Edenton"[7] located in Chowan County in northeastern North Carolina.

Reared in northeastern Pennsylvania among immigrants from many different European countries, we Patiences knew we were not alone in having ancestors who became brand-new by casting off former lives, some perhaps by changing surnames. Might that be what the 17-year-old Crowder had done in 1863? If so, what had his surname been before, should he have had one, since many enslaved persons did not?

Had the first generation of Patience children been curious about their father's family, but too hesitant or too respectful to ask? What might Crowder, that proud Colored[8] citizen of West Pittston, Pennsylvania, have told them and his much younger free-born wife, Elsie, about his former life in N.C.? I suspect very little.[9]

Three generations later, this Patience descendant has found the answers to a few of those questions. I know that Crowder had shared some details of his former life with at least two of his grandsons. When a 1928 newspaper article[10] was published about him two years prior to his death, most of his grandchildren already were adults; therefore, I have no idea if the article provided anything new for them. It does, however, provide pertinent information for future curious generations.

Grandpa had died two years before I was born, so I never had the opportunity to be in his presence; but I was very much aware of his existence. When I was just a little girl, his daughter, Lillian, with no children of her own, would spend many a quiet Sabbath afternoon with me following morning church services and the filling mid-day dinners.

Some people chose to nap on quiet Sundays when most labor would cease, but Aunt Lillie delighted in perusing the black and white photographs she had so meticulously inserted in her red velvet-covered album.

Lillian Maria Patience Cuff
(author's collection)

Someone with a Brownie camera had enjoyed snapping photographs of relatives and friends who congregated at the Patience homestead. During the first quarter of the 20th century, members of the Patience clan began exiting our small borough for better job opportunities. But when they would motor back home, especially on Sundays, they always made it a point to pay Grandma Patience a visit. They knew she would have baked several of her delicious pies the previous day, apple being her favorite.

"Never know who might be stopping by for a visit," she would anticipate. After her husband's death in 1930, Grandma Patience became more and more reclusive. Attacks of rheumatism [arthritis] required her to use a cane for navigating her home and yard. She would pass away in 1940 at the age of eighty-four.

Her daughter, Lillian, at age ninety-one moved from Pennsylvania to New Jersey in 1974 to live with my family for the last twelve years of her life. Close friends and relatives would travel to my backyard patio to celebrate the birthdays of a delightful lady addressed as "Aunt Lillie" by many, biologically related or not.

Her precious red velvet-covered photograph album and other belongings remained in my home after her death in 1986. Included was a black tin document box in which she had stored her father's Civil War records and other treasured mementoes.

Four Generations Celebrate Aunt Lillie's 98th Birthday [11]
(author's collection)

Juanita Patience Moss, left, and her great aunt Lillian Patience Cuff look over Miss Cuff's 100th birthday cake in their Montclair home. They are making a wish—probably for many more birthdays.

Aunt Lillie's 100th Birthday Party

July 12, 1983

(author's collection)

Juanita Patience Moss, left, and her great aunt Lillian Patience Cuff look over Miss Cuff's birthday cake in their Montclair home. They are making a wish— probably for many more birthdays.

Montclair Times

CHAPTER 2
WHAT'S IN A NAME?

Not until the spring of 1998 would I have any compelling reason to examine Grandpa's military records. I would do so because I was in need of proof that he had served in the Union Army during the Civil War.

A new monument was to be unveiled on July 18, 1998, in Washington, D.C., to honor Black Union soldiers and sailors. Surrounding it would be a wall with their names inscribed on steel plates. Prior to the event, the *Washington Post* had suggested that descendants search the National Parks Database to verify the spelling of their Civil War ancestors' names. When I searched for the name "Crowder Patience," the response, however, was, *"No known soldier."*

"How can that be?" I was flabbergasted. "Why, I can take any naysayer straight to Grandpa's grave in the West Pittston Cemetery."

Pvt. Crowder Patience
103rd Pennsylvania
Company C

(courtesy of Philip Dente)

West Pittston, Pennsylvania

I was remembering that for decades a Patience tradition had been for family members to gather on Decoration Day (now Memorial Day)[12] to attend the annual parade, and then follow the band to the cemetery where the war-dead were honored by rifles volleying, cannons booming, and "Taps" sounding. Townsfolk would carry bunches of flowers for decorating family graves. To this day, my Civil War ancestor's gravesite can be located easily by its Union tombstone, G.A.R.[13] stanchion and American flag.

Also, I was remembering that after Grandpa had died, on each Decoration Day a large American flag would be hooked across the length of my great-grandmother's heavily shaded vine-covered porch. That flag was the very same one draping Grandpa's coffin at his military funeral on February 4, 1930.[14]

Finally, I remembered Grandpa's military records in Aunt Lillie's tin document box. I had never read the discharge certificate before, having had little interest in Civil War battles and personalities—only its outcome. Although I had placed flowers on Grandpa's gravesite, I could not recall his regiment's name and because I was living in Virginia, I could not check out his tombstone.

No need, though, for on his discharge record I found Grandpa's regiment—the 103rd PA Volunteers. A big surprise for me, however, was in finding Grandpa's surname spelled "Pacien."

CHAPTER 3

PVT. CROWDER PACIEN THE SOLDIER

My great grandfather enlisted in the Union Army on January 1, 1864, at Plymouth, N.C. Before the war, it had been a lovely ante bellum port near the mouth of the Roanoke River in northeastern N.C. Now nine Union regiments were garrisoned there to block Confederate communication with Richmond, Virginia, and, also, to block access to the Atlantic Ocean so the South could not exchange tobacco and cotton for European munitions.

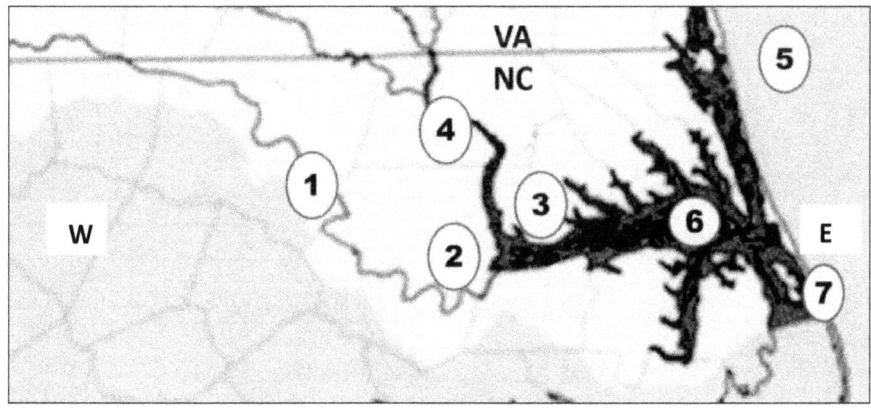

MAP OF THE ALBEMARLE SOUND

1. Roanoke River
2. Plymouth
3. Edenton
4. Chowan River

5. Atlantic Ocean
6. Albemarle Sound
7. Roanoke Island

(author's legend)

| P. | 103 | Pa. |

Crowder Pacien

Appears with rank of ....Reg'd. Cook.... on

Muster and Descriptive Roll of a Detachment of U. S. Vols. forwarded

for the ..103.. Reg't Pa. Infantry. Roll dated Plymouth, N.C., Apr. 4, 1864.

Where born .....Chowan Co. N.C....

Age 18 y'rs; occupation ...Laborer...

When enlisted ......Jan. 1......, 1864.

Where enlisted ......Plymouth N.C......

For what period enlisted ......3...... years.

Eyes ...Black...; hair ...Black...

Complexion ...Black...; height ..5.. ft. ..5.. in.

When mustered in ......April 4......, 1864.

Where mustered in ......Plymouth N.C......

Bounty paid $ ....100...; due $ ....100....

Where credited ....

Company to which assigned ......C......

Remarks: Enlisted in accordance with G.O. 73 (Oct.) Sec. 10 series 1863 from War Dept.

Pvt. Crowder Pacien's Enlistment Record
January 1, 1864
National Archives

| P. | 103 | Pa. |

Croder Pacien

Pr., Co. C 103 Reg't Pa. Infantry.

Appears on

Company Descriptive Book

of the organization named above.

DESCRIPTION.

Age 18 years; height 5 feet 5 inches.
Complexion Black
Eyes Black; hair Black
Where born Chowan Co. N.C.,
Occupation Laborer

ENLISTMENT.

When Jan 1, 186 4.
Where Plymouth, N.C.,
By whom Capt Modurus; term 3 y'rs.
Remarks: Colored Cook

Pvt. Croder Pacien in Company C Descriptive Book
January 1, 1864

Roanoke Island provided a natural blockade at the mouth of the Albemarle Sound where the southern flowing Roanoke River empties. Every six months each Union regiment garrisoned at Plymouth would detach one company to Roanoke Island. When Crowder Pacien enlisted, he was assigned to the 103rd PA's "Co. C" whose turn was next to sail from Plymouth to Roanoke Island.

Pvt. Crowder Pacien's Company Muster Roll for Jan. & Feb. 1864

National Archives

Across the Sound, "Co. F" was waiting impatiently to sail back to Plymouth just as soon as "Co. C" would arrive on January 2nd to replace it. The men of "Co. F" were eagerly anticipating their return to a place where life would be much less monotonous than what they had been experiencing for the last six months on "dull" Roanoke Island.[15] Three months later, however, on the lovely spring Sunday afternoon of April 17, 1864, the Rebels would surprise these Yankees while they were preparing for their weekly dress parade.

By April 20th the Union soldiers at Plymouth had been defeated soundly. The brand-new ironclad *CSS Albemarle*,[16] built specifically for navigating the narrow Roanoke River, was critical to the Confederate victory.

For several months, the Yankees had been hearing rumors about a ship being built miles upriver from Plymouth. Because Roanoke Island was in Yankee possession farther south, the Union troops garrisoned at Plymouth were confident that no enemy ships would be able to reach them. Consequently, those soldiers felt quite safe—that is, until April 17th when they heard the warning shots of pickets on duty, followed by the frantic yells, *"The Rebs are coming!"*

An estimated 150 Yankees would be killed during the four-day battle [April 17-20, 1864]. The wounded were held captive at Plymouth while the more "hale and hearty" were escorted further south by train to the abominable Andersonville Prison in Georgia.[17]

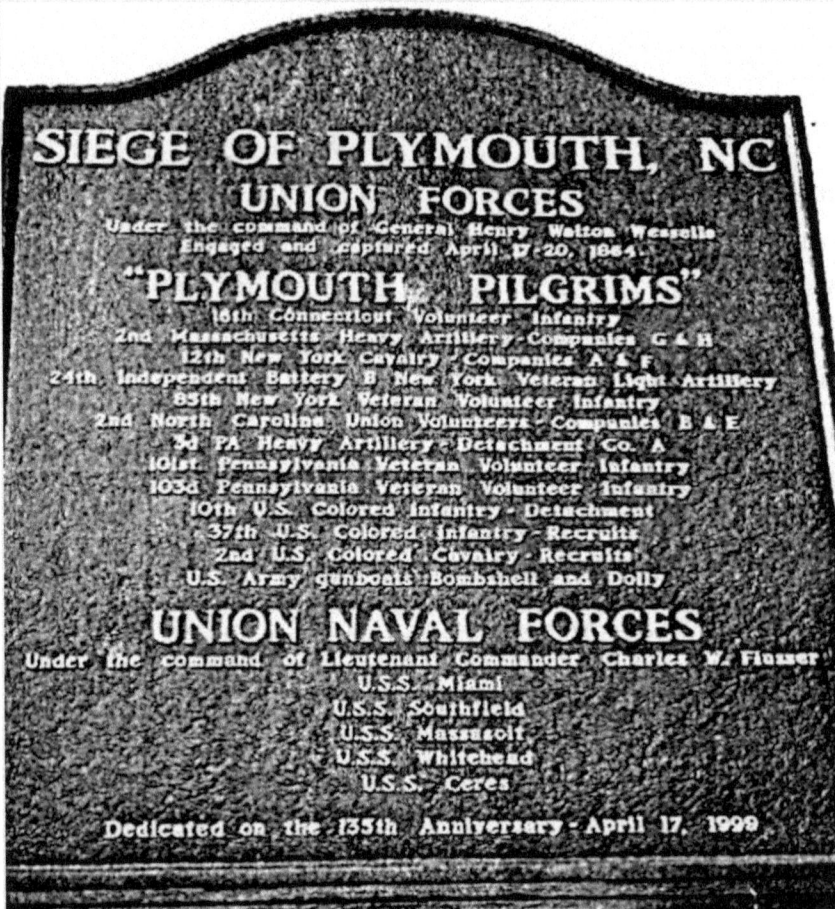

Siege of Plymouth, N.C. Historic Marker"[18]
April 17-20, 1864
(author's collection)

Scholars have yet to agree on the fate of all thirteen Black cooks who had been enlisted as privates in four of the nine Union regiments garrisoned at Plymouth prior to the devastating battle. Neither is it known what happened to all of the Black recruits who were waiting there to be mustered into their respective regiments. [19]

Among those fortunately accounted for, though, was my great grandfather. Recorded in the *Regimental Roster 103rd PA Volunteers*: *"Pacien, Crowder, Company C, mustered age 18, April 4, 1864-June 25, 1865. Cook, Afro-American, apparently escaped capture following the Battle of Plymouth, North Carolina, on April 20, 1864."*[20]

How had he been able to escape capture? A known fact is that he would not have been taken to Andersonville with the "Plymouth Pilgrims."[21] Confederate orders were that captured Blacks were to be remanded back to slavery.[22] Slaves were chattel—valuable property to be returned to their masters, that is, if not killed under the black flag order of *"No quarter."*[23]

The answer to how eighteen-year-old Pvt. Crowder Pacien had been able to escape capture is that he was safely detached on Roanoke Island with "Co. C." It was to be the unfortunate fate of the 103rd PA's "Co. F" to "face the elephant"[24] at Plymouth, to be captured, and to suffer horrendously, with many succumbing to then untreatable diseases at Andersonville Prison before the war ceased a year later.

P.C.ˣ | 103 | Pa.

Pacien ˣ Crowder

Put., Co. C, 103 Reg't Pennsylvania Inf.

Appears on

Company Muster Roll

for *March & April*, 1864.

Joined for duty and enrolled:

When *Jany 1*, 1864.*
Where *Plymouth N. C.* *
Period *3* years.*

Present or absent *Present.*
Stoppage, $ 100 for
Due Gov't, $ 100 for
Remarks: *On daily duty assistant cook (Colored)*

ˣ *Corrected by Carter* &c.

* ☞ See enrollment on card from muster-in roll.

Book mark:

Pvt. Crowder Pacien Company Muster Roll for Mar. & Apr. 1864

National Archives

| P | 103 | Pa. |

Crowder Pacien
Colord UnderCook. Co. C.
Pvt., Co. C., 103 Reg't Pennsylvania Inf.

Appears on **Returns** as follows:

Feb'y 1864 (Colored Under Cook)
Gain: Enlisted in the Reg't Jan 1 '64
Roanoke Isld –
(Asst Cook)

Apl. 1864 to May 1865:
On duty Assistant
Colored Under Cook.
(Pvt. Co. C.)

Name appears also as
Cowdien Pacien
Crowder Pacie

Book mark:

(546)   J. W. Elliott
                          Copyist.

Pvt. Crowder Pacien Detached To Roanoke Island

National Archives

According to the *History of the 103rd Pennsylvania Regiment*,[25] when the war was over, Crowder Pacien travelled with his regiment to Pennsylvania where he had never been before. On July 13, 1865, the 103rd Pennsylvania Volunteer Regiment received its discharge and final payment on the steps of the Courthouse in Harrisburg, the State Capitol.

Afterwards, Crowder's comrades set off for their respective homes in northwestern Pennsylvania where they had enlisted four years prior. Sadly, though, a high percentage of the original number had been killed at Plymouth or died in Confederate prisons, including those at Andersonville, Charleston and Florence. For that reason, the 103rd PA was dubbed "The Hardship Regiment."[26]

After receiving his final pay, young Crowder Pacien was faced with a major decision concerning his future. At last a free man, he could make choices about what he wanted to do with his own life. Should he return to Edenton, North Carolina, and back to the known lifestyle of laboring in the fields, even though for wages now? Or should he remain in far-away Pennsylvania to face the unknown all alone?

| P | 103 | Pa. |

Crowder Pacien

Priv., Co. G, 103 Reg't Pennsylvania Inf.

Age 18 years.

Appears on **Co. Muster-out Roll,** dated

New Berne N C June 25, 1865

Muster-out to date June 25, 1865

Last paid to Aug 31, 1864.

Clothing account:

Last settled Never, 186 ; drawn since $ 100

Due soldier $ 100; due U. S. $ 100

Am't for cloth'g in kind or money adv'd $ 46 52/100

Due U. S. for arms, equipments, &c., $ 100

Bounty paid $ 100; due $ 100

Remarks: Assistant under cook (colored)

Pvt. Crowder Pacien's Co. Muster-Out

National Archives

CERTIFICATE IN LIEU OF LOST OR DESTROYED DISCHARGE CERTIFICATE

To all Whom it May Concern:

Know ye, That *Crowder Pacien* *Private* of Company *C.* *One hundred and third* Regiment of *Pennsylvania Infantry* VOLUNTEERS, who was *enrolled* on the *first* day of *January*, one thousand eight hundred and *sixty-four*, to serve *three* years was Discharged from the service of the United States on the *twenty-fifth* day of *June*, one thousand eight hundred and *sixty-five* by reason of *muster out of company.*

This Certificate is given under the provisions of the Act of Congress approved July 1, 1902, "to authorize the Secretary of War to furnish certificates in lieu of lost or destroyed discharges," to honorably discharged officers or enlisted men or their widows, upon evidence that the original discharge certificate has been lost or destroyed, and upon the condition imposed by said Act, that this certificate "shall not be accepted as a voucher for the payment of any claim against the United States for pay, bounty, or other allowances, or as evidence in any other case."

Given at the War Department, Washington, D. C., this *fourth* day of *June*, one thousand nine hundred and *twelve*.

By authority of the Secretary of War:

Adjutant General.

(A. G. O. 150)

1919513

Pvt. Crowder Pacien's Discharge Certificate

(Lillian Patience Cuff's collection)

To read content easily, go to next page.

DISCHARGE CERTIFICATE

To all Whom it May Concern:

"Know ye, That <u>Crowder Pacien</u>, <u>Private of Company C</u>, <u>One hundred and third</u> <u>Regiment of Pennsylvania Infantry</u> VOLUNTEER who was <u>enrolled</u> on the <u>first</u> day of <u>January,</u> one <u>thousand eight hundred</u> and <u>sixty-four,</u> to serve <u>three years</u> was <u>discharged</u> from the service of the United States on the <u>twenty-fifth</u> day of <u>June</u>, one thousand <u>eight hundred</u> and <u>sixty-five</u> by reason of <u>muster out of company.</u>

This certificate is given under the Act of Congress approved July 1, 1902, "to authorize the Secretary of War to furnish certificate in lieu of loss or destroyed discharge" to honorably discharged officers or enlisted men or their widows, after evidence that the assigned discharge certificate has been lost or destroyed and upon condition imposed by said Act that the certificate shall not be accepted as a voucher for the payment of any claim against the United States for pay, bounty or other allowances, or as evidence in any other case.

Given at the War Department, Washington, D.C., this <u>fourth</u> day of <u>June</u> one thousand nine hundred and <u>twelve.</u>

By authority of the Secretary of War :"

...

<u>Pvt. Crowder Pacien's Discharge Certificate</u>

Crowder Pacien would make the decision to remain in Pennsylvania, known as the "Keystone State."

KEYSTONE STATE ANTHRACITE COAL PLAQUE

COMMONWEALTH OF PENNSYLVANIA

Carved by Charles Edgar Patience[27]

Grandson of Crowder and Elsie Patience

(author's collection)

CHAPTER 4
CROWDER PATIENCE THE CITIZEN

Crowder Patience Standing Soldier-Straight at Age 81
West Pittston, Pennsylvania
ca. 1928
(Lillian Patience Cuff's collection)

Five years following the war, the 1870 Federal census would count twenty-three-year-old "Croder" Patience as living in Mt. Holley, Penna., and married to nineteen-year-old Emma. Presumably, she passed away young since Crowder would marry sixteen-year-old Elsie Veden in Mechanicsburg, Penna., on August 4, 1874. [28]

Being an experienced and industrious laborer, he was hired by local farmers in southwestern Pennsylvania to work their fields during the summer months. Because Crowder enjoyed working with horses more and wanted steadier work, he found employment with a horse breeder near Harrisburg. One of his jobs was to deliver colts to their purchasers. On one trip, when travelling over the rugged mountain ranges and down into the lush Wyoming Valley in northeastern Pennsylvania, he decided to someday plant new roots there.

Several years later, Crowder would relocate his growing family to the Wyoming Valley. Eons ago, it had been carved out of the high Appalachian ranges by the southern flowing Susquehanna River. Once tranquil, the area had become the bustling hub of the anthracite coal mining industry during the latter 18th Century.

The Patience name in later years would become well known there due to the anthracite coal novelty business of Crowder and Elsie's first son. The unique art of "Harry B. Patience and Sons" was displayed in 2016 at the new National Museum of African American History and Culture (NMAAHC) in Washington, D.C.

A small gleaming anthracite coal heart[29] can be admired in a glass display case on a wall of the first Concourse Level. The heart was the Patience signature piece to be worn on a chain encircling a lady's neck. Also, in the same collectors' display case is a pair of Harry's vintage needle-nose pliers as well a rectangular copper-covered wooden board he had used for printing his catalog of unique coal items.

Business Card[30]
ca. 1932
(author's collection)

Throughout the years, gems of information about my forebears have become embedded in my mind due to my having been such an inquisitive child who was always asking questions. To many of them, Aunt Lillie's response had been, *"Juanita, we just didn't ask our parents things like that."* Later, though, she just might provide something to satisfy my curiosity—at least for a little while.

Her parents had thought it fit, though, to disclose where each had lived as children: Crowder, as a slave on a plantation near Edenton, North Carolina, and Elsie, although freeborn, as a "bound" girl[31] in Dillsburg, Pennsylvania.

Their eight children knew where each had been born. Unlike their father, they also knew their exact birthdates. Even though Elsie could neither read nor write, she had asked someone to record all vital Patience family information in her small *Bible*—marriages, births, and deaths. The earliest entries were written neatly by an adult, but the later ones were recorded in a childish scrawl, perhaps Florence's, since she was the eldest.

All of the children certainly were well aware that their father had been a Civil War soldier because they had seen him every year in the town's Decoration Day Parade. He would march proudly alongside his Civil War G.A.R. comrades clad in their natty navy blue suits. In later years, also marching with them would be the younger Spanish-American War veterans.

ACT OF MAY 11, 1912.

No. 1,140,513

Reissue

UNITED STATES OF AMERICA

DEPARTMENT of the INTERIOR

≻ BUREAU OF PENSIONS ≺

It is hereby certified That, in conformity with the laws of the United States _____ Crowder Patient _____ who was a Private Co. C, 103rd Regiment Pennsylvania Infantry _____ is entitled to a pension at the rate of _____ Sixteen _____ dollars per month, to commence June 6, 1912 and Twenty dollars per month from December 25, 1913 and Twenty-four dollars per month from December 25, 1918.

Given at the Department of the Interior this twenty-sixth day of March one thousand nine hundred and thirteen and of the Independence of the United States of America the one hundred and thirty-seventh

Secretary of the Interior

Countersigned

Former payments covering any portion of the same time to be deducted

<u>*Veteran Crowder Patient's Pension Increase*</u>

Act of May 11, 1912

National Archives

Perhaps not much else about Crowder's past was shared because most children of ex-slaves were not interested in learning anything at all about their parents' lives in bondage.³² Neither did the parents have any desire to recollect bitter memories concerning their former lives. They chose simply to forget pasts far too degrading for remembering, and certainly for relating.

Far distanced from the South, and one of only a few Colored families in our small borough of West Pittston, the first generation of Patience children were reared in an ethnically diverse community to which many European men had migrated to work in the anthracite³³ coal mines. Crowder Patience never became a coal miner, for he was a toiler of the soil—a farmer and a gardener. In addition, for many years he drove a team of horses to deliver produce grown by his employers.

Crowder Patience With G.A.R. Comrades On Decoration Day
2ⁿᵈ row – [at center] 5ᵗʰ from left
ca. 1913
(courtesy of Robert Nardone)

The Patience children attended the public schools with white children and were members of the First Presbyterian Church until St. Mark's African American Episcopal (A.M.E.) Church was built in West Pittston in 1906. My Grandfather Harry was instrumental in building the church and served as the Sunday School Superintendent. By that time, the first generation of Patience children were married adults. For many years afterwards, the Sunday School instructed the numerous grandchildren of Crowder and Elsie Patience.[34]

Seemingly, Aunt Lillie knew nothing about her father's relatives in Edenton, N.C. When I asked her about them, she said that her father had never spoken of any. Members of that freeborn second generation seemed not to have any burning desire to trace their father's origins in the segregated South. First, they had heard too many horror stories about how Colored people were mistreated there. Second, North Carolina was very distant from Pennsylvania and third, they did not know any relatives to contact there. So, why would they want to go? One of the younger sons, Chester Douglas, would be the first Patience descendent to cross the Mason-Dixon Line[35] to travel south when he left home in 1910 to attend Howard University in Washington, D.C.

Members of the third generation would begin to develop an interest in their ancestry during the first quarter of the 20th century. As students of the West

Pittston Public School System, they had studied United States history which included nothing positive about Colored people. I am aware that two of my Grandfather Harry's sons, Robert and Kenneth, had asked questions of their grandfather.

Proof of Uncle Bob's curiosity is at the National Archives in Washington, D.C., where his signature can be seen on a research permit dated two years after his grandfather's death in 1930. Uncle Bob was the first non-archivist to research the military records of Private Crowder Patience, 103rd Pennsylvania Volunteers "Co. C" and seventy years later in 2000, I was the second.

Sometime in the 1970s when Uncle Bob was visiting from his home in Philadelphia, Pa., he surprised me with a copy of a *Sunday Independent* newspaper article about Grandpa. Uncle Bob somehow must have discerned that in the future I just might become the family griot, perhaps because I was the kid always asking questions of the grownups.

The article had been written just prior to Memorial Day in 1928. I was thrilled to receive it, even though I could not see Grandpa's photograph clearly. Regardless, the piece provided the framework on which I would build my novel, *Created to Be Free,* some forty years later.

The title of the article is *"Civil War Veteran of Unusual Career is Valley Resident."* A subtitle follows with *"Crowder Pacient Lived in Slavery Before the Emancipation Proclamation of President Lincoln and When Opportunity Permitted He Joined Forces With His Deliverer."* [36]

Excerpts:

KEEN IN RECOLLECTIONS

"Few days of the year carry more meaning with them than Memorial Day. Once in each twelve months it is observed and throughout the land the disappearing ranks of the Blue and Gray form the line for the parade of honor to their departed comrades. Sixty-three years have passed since the last shots of the great Civil War were fired and few of the heroes remain.

As the lines are formed this year and the veterans grouped in the cars which will carry them along the line of march, to no one present will such a stream of memories return as to one wearer of the Blue from Exeter. To no other man in Wyoming Valley has such a great wealth and variety of experiences been vouchsafed.

An old and respected colored man is the one in mind. Now eighty-two years of age, a slave in the South before the war, a soldier in the Union Army, a farmer of old Wyoming Valley, and a man who has held only two positions—both of trust—for the past sixty years, who else could hold such a position in life here? Crowder Pacient is the name of this respected resident….

Up until two years ago Pacient worked steadily for the Carpenter family, one of the original settlers of that part of the Valley. He came to the family, to the partnership of Jesse and Isaac Carpenter, in the fall of 1883. Work with horses is connected with his entire life. Two years ago, after going back to work too soon after a siege of pneumonia his need of a rest became apparent, his team of horses was shot and he, in his forty-fifth year with the Carpenter family is an honored retainer whose loyal services are respected….

He has kept up his active membership in the G.A.R., attends the meetings whenever able to do so, meets his old comrades of the war regularly and hopes to be able to take part in the Memorial Day parade this year. He wasn't sure he could but he was going to try hard. His place would be hard to fill and he will be sorely missed if not there."

****

Using improved genealogical tools, other members of the fourth generation have become griots, also. For instance, LeRoy Crowder Patience Jr. and Virginia Smith Monterio both used *Ancestry.com* for tracing Patience roots to Cameroon. Marian Patience Henry, like our great-Aunt Lillie, is the creator of beautiful family albums. Several other Patience descendants have become their branch's genealogists, as well.

My first cousin Katherine Patience Kennedy, for instance, adds an interesting anecdote to our family lore. She states that her father told her that his grandfather's owner was a Frenchman from the West Indies. To be privy to such a French connection, Uncle Kenneth had to have heard it directly from his grandfather Crowder.

Years later during my sleuthing, I would discover the possible French connection. Francois Briols, a Frenchman from the Caribbean island of Guadaloupe, had been the owner of the Briols plantation in Edenton, N.C., from 1796 to 1803.[37] Might that be the plantation from which our Patience ancestor would abscond sixty years later?

Oral history easily can become folklore and with each successive story teller, may become embellished. Perhaps that is true with our family, such as Uncle Bob's speculation that Grandpa may have been given the name "Patience" when he enlisted in the Union Army because he was so patient. Also, according to Uncle Bob, Grandpa had said his master called him "Tobe."

It would not be folklore, though, to suggest that the young "Tobe" matched John Hope Franklin's description of a typical absconding slave in *Runaway Slaves: Rebels on the Plantation.* "Young men in their teens and twenties…described as having dark complexion…"[38] When studying Grandpa's photo[39] when he was old, I easily can imagine how he may have looked when he was a dark-skinned teen-aged field hand.

The truths I know about Crowder Pacien [Patience], I included under "Facts" in my novel.[40] His military records state that he was born in Chowan County, North Carolina, about which I knew absolutely nothing. When I began writing, I was not familiar even with the story of Harriet Jacobs,[41] the Edenton slave girl who had hidden for seven years in her free grandmother's attic to avoid the nonconsensual advances of her much older master.

To get a feel for the environment of northeastern North Carolina, I needed to make a trip there to study the terrain during October. Why October? Since my great grandfather had enlisted in a January, possibly he may have absconded several months before. October would have been the perfect time for running. The harvesting was completed, the nights had grown longer, and the temperatures had not dropped cold yet.

Crowder Patience's life's journey would carry him from the sweet potato fields of northeastern North Carolina where he was born to the anthracite coal fields of northeastern Pennsylvania where he was buried. His journey would carry him from bondage to freedom— from slave to respected citizen.

<u>Compilation of Crowder Patience</u>

With Discharge Certificate and American Flag

Created by Artist Joseph Mills

For a student project a Bowie State University

Bowie, Maryland

2009

Crowder Patience's Death Certificate

Birthplace	North Carolina
Date of death	January 30, 1930
Cause of death	Apoplexy [42], cold & grippe [43]
Date of burial	February 3, 1930
Place of burial	West Pittston Cemetery

(Lillian Patience Cuff's collection)

CROWDER PATIENCE CIVIL WAR VETERAN DIES [44]

"Crowder Patience, aged 83 years, a resident of West Pittston for many years and widely known as a veteran soldier of the Civil War, passed away yesterday afternoon at 3:35 o'clock at his home, 828 Luzerne Avenue. Though advanced in years, Mr. Patience had enjoyed good health and was able to get around his home until one week ago, when he was stricken and took to his bed. His condition had been very serious during this past few days.

Mr. Patience was born in Edington, North Carolina on Dec. 25, 1848. His early life was spent in his native state. On Jan. 1, 1864, he enlisted as a soldier in the Union Army, and served with credit until the close of the war, having been mustered out of the service on June 25, 1865.

Since shortly after the war Mr. Patience had been a resident of West Pittston and was held in high esteem by many friends for his sterling character and his industrious nature. Until his retirement three years ago he was employed by the J. B. Carpenter Estate for many years. He was the father of Harry B. Patience, who conducted a coal novelty business in West Pittston until his death in 1926. Mr. Patience has been a member of the West Pittston Presbyterian Church for many years.

The survivors are his widow and the following sons and daughters: Ms. W. K. Glover and Mrs. S. P. Lee of West Pittston; Mrs. C. E. Cuff of Pittsburgh, wife of the evangelist who is at present conducting meetings in the Italian Presbyterian Church on Parsonage Street; Mrs. N. T. Garrett of West Pittston; C. D. Patience of Washington, D.C.; and Percy Patience of West Pittston. Twenty-one grandchildren and nine great-grandchildren also survive.

The funeral services will be conducted at the home Monday afternoon at 2:30 o'clock by Rev. Dr. Thomas Swan. Burial will be in the West Pittston Cemetery."

CROWDER PATIENCE IS BURIED WITH FULL MILITARY HONORS [45]

Full military honors were accorded Crowder Patience, a Civil War veteran, whose funeral was held at 2:30 o'clock yesterday afternoon from the home, 828 Luzerne avenue. Three veterans of the Civil War and a detail of Spanish-American war veterans were in attendance at the services at the home and at the grave. The casket was draped with the American flag.

Rev. Dr. Thomas W. Swan, pastor of the First Presbyterian Church, conducted the services. The profusion of lovely flowers and the many friends in attendance bore evidence of the respect in which Mr. Patience was held.

At West Pittston cemetery, where burial was made, a detail of Spanish-American war veterans, commanded by Chief of Police M. P. McHale, of Pittston, fired a volley over the grave and taps were sounded by John Reid.

The pall bearers, all grandsons of deceased were: Walter J. Glover, Jr., Kenneth V. Patience, C. Edward Glover, Wilmer Patience, Miles R. Glover and Harold Patience.

(photo by Philip Dente)
2018

<u>**Union Tombstone of Pvt. Crowder Patience**</u>

103rd Pennsylvania Volunteers
Company C

with
G.A.R. Stanchion and American Flag

Elsie Veden Patience
Wife

West Pittston Cemetery
West Pittston, Pennsylvania

Application for Military Headstone

For Pvt. Crowder Pacien/Patient/Patience

(Lillian Patience Cuff's collection))

NAME						(3-P.A. 1a)
Patient, Crowder						ACT OF JULY 3, 1926
Certificate No. 1140513		ARMY INVALID		Law: Act of May 1, 1920		
Service Pt C 103 Pa						
Disability						

CLASS	RATE	DATE OF COMMENCEMENT	DATE OF CERTIFICATE	Homes—Admitted
	50	May 1, 1920		Discharged
	65	Aug. 4, 1926		Died Jany 30, 1930 Reported FEB 13 1930

Jany 30, 1930 Accrued and/or ... APR 14 1930
Payable to widow Elsie V Patient

828 Luzerne Ave.
West Pittston
Pa.

Widow's Pension for Elsie Veden Patient

April 14, 1930

(courtesy of Joseph Lawrence Jr.)

THE NATIONAL CIVIL WAR MUSEUM

Respectfully Honors
The
Memory
And
Military Service
Of

**CROWDER PACIEN
CO C 103RD REGT
PA VOL INF US**

During the American Civil War, 1861 - 1865. In recognition of his selfless devotion to duty, this Veteran's personal service is commemorated on The Walk of Valor, at The National Civil War Museum, Harrisburg, Pennsylvania.

Recognized on this day of December 15, 2000

GEORGE E. HICKS, Chief Executive Officer

National Civil War Museum Brick Commemoration [46]
Walk of Valor

Harrisburg, Pennsylvania

(author's collection)

"Spirit of Freedom"
Washington, D.C.

CHAPTER 5

LEARNING ABOUT BLACK SOLDIERS IN THE CIVIL WAR

My unexpected Civil War research would begin after I had attended the unveiling of the bronze monument "Spirit of Freedom" in Washington, D.C., on July 18, 1998. It was created to honor the U.S.C.T. (United States Colored Troops) and other Black soldiers who had served the Union during the Civil War. Just recently, I had learned that a particular category of Black soldier was not being recognized by the memorial—those who had served in white regiments and not in the segregated Black ones.

My great-grandfather, Pvt. Crowder Patience, was such a soldier. He had enlisted under General Orders 323[47] that allowed men of African descent to be recruited as undercooks and ranked as privates. They were promised that should the war be won by the Union, like all other veterans they would be eligible to apply for an invalid [disability] government pension. Once mustered-in as undercooks, some, however, were assigned to other jobs according to their skills, for example as teamsters,[48] farriers,[49] blacksmiths[50], and saddlers.[51] Many other Blacks, including Medal of Honor recipient Pvt. Bruce Anderson[52] of the 142nd NY Infantry, enlisted in the regular Army and not under General Orders 323.

At a symposium for Civil War descendants attending the unveiling of the "Spirit of Freedom" in July 1998, I learned the reason why the names of those Black soldiers are not inscribed on the Wall of Honor, not even the name of Medal of Honor recipient Pvt. Bruce Anderson. I also learned that many Civil War scholars were unaware that Black soldiers had served in white regiments. Or if certain scholars were aware, they disparaged the roles of those particular soldiers if they were not proven combatants. In fact, several historians told me that, indeed, it was a known fact that some Colored men had served in white regiments, but only by passing as Caucasians.

That may have been true of some, but not my identifiably Black great-grandfather, Pvt. Crowder Pacien, who was not passing for anything but "Col'd" as is recorded on his military records. Therefore, I formed the following hypothesis: *If there had been one, there may have been more.* And there were.

Information concerning that particular category of Black soldier was difficult to find. Only because my ancestor is one of those forgotten, was I privy to have knowledge of Blacks serving in white regiments during the Civil War. In the 2004 publication of a small tome entitled *Forgotten Black Soldiers in White Regiments During the Civil War,* I listed the names of 1,000 cooks and undercooks I found on the rosters of thirteen of the twenty-three Union states.

Even though I knew it to be an incomplete list, for my personal satisfaction, 1,000 names were more than sufficient to support my hypothesis. With that number I had filled a hypothetical regiment of Black soldiers while adding an actual 1,000 to the estimated 179,000 Black soldiers who had served the Union. [53]

Encouraged by my publisher, Craig Scott of Heritage Books, I later researched the remaining Union States as well as the "Unionist" [54] regiments organized in Confederate States. I found over 1,500 more names and not only of cooks, but of many who had served in other capacities as well. My lists remain incomplete because still more names of the formerly forgotten Black soldiers may be retrieved from the National Archives and/or *Ancestry.com*.[55] Perhaps someday they will be by other descendants searching for their ancestors or by interested Civil War "buffs."

In conclusion then, the reason for Pvt. Crowder Patience's name not being inscribed on the Wall of Honor surrounding the "Spirit of Freedom" monument in Washington, D.C., is that he had not served in one of the segregated regiments such as the 54th MA, 55th MA, 5th MA (Col'd) Cavalry, 29th Conn., or the USCT.

The name of Samuel Patterson, grandfather of my stepmother, Alice Patterson Patience, however, is inscribed on the Wall. He was a 20-year-old freeborn man living in Berwick, Pennsylvania, when President Abraham Lincoln finally permitted Blacks to join the Union Army per General Orders 143.[56] Samuel James Patterson would heed the call and traveled to Massachusetts to enlist in the 5th MA (Col'd) Cavalry.

When the "Spirit of Freedom" monument was unveiled on July 18, 1998, the Wall of Honor had not yet been completed. It would be at a later date. Four years after its dedication, Christine Patterson, great-granddaughter of Samuel James Patterson, was in Washington for business. She asked if I would escort her to the monument so she might see her ancestor's name inscribed on the Wall of Honor. I was happy to oblige.

CHAPTER 6

PVT. THOMAS PATIENCE'S NAME ON THE WALL OF HONOR

Christine and I rode the Metro from Alexandria, Virginia, to the Shaw Station in D.C. and then escalated up into the bright sunlight. Immediately greeting our eyes as our feet rolled off the last step, was the magnificent bronze monument created by Ed Hamilton.[57] Inscribed with 209,145 names of Black soldiers and their white officers, the Wall of Honor surrounds the "Spirit of Freedom" monument on three sides.

After finding the 5th MA (Col'd) Cavalry and locating the name of Christine's ancestor, Samuel Patterson, my eyes began perusing other names on the Wall. When moving to the left, what did my wandering eyes behold? It was the name of Thomas Patience, also a member of the 5th Massachusetts (Col'd) Cavalry.

> Mills Moore ★ Richard H. Moore ★ Thomas H. Moore ★ Sylvester Moores ★ Charles H. Moran ★ George E
> orris ★ James Morse ★ John Mortimer ★ George Morton ★ George W. Morton ★ John Morton ★ Antonio
> hy ★ Frank Murray ★ James A. Murray ★ Shadreck Murray ★ William H. Murrey ★ Ephraim Myers ★ Isaac My
> ★ Frank Nelson ★ Isaac Nelson ★ John Nelson ★ Luther Nelson ★ Philip Nelson ★ Preston Nelson ★ Teri
>
> ## ★ Thomas Patience ★
>
> Postles ★ John W. Postles ★ Dashbrook Potter ★ John A. Poulston ★ Horace M. Powers ★ Reuben B. Pra
> tchard ★ Ross Proctor ★ Thomas Proctor ★ Thomas S. Proctor ★ Henry H. Profit ★ Rhodes H. Prophe
> ffe ★ Warren Ray ★ James S. Raymond ★ Oxford Reddy ★ Hiram W. Reed ★ James Reed ★ Warwick Reed ★ E
> Richardson ★ Charles Richardson ★ Francis Richardson ★ John H. Richardson ★ Luke Richardson ★ Robert R
> Roberson ★ Henry Robert ★ George Roberts ★ John Roberts ★ Thomas Roberts ★ Thomas Robins ★ Charles Ro
> Rodgers ★ Joshua Rodman ★ Albert M. Rogers ★ George A. Rogers ★ Henry M. Rogers ★ James Rogers ★ J
> ★ Henry S. Russell ★ Jacob Russell ★ James E. Russell ★ Moses Russell ★ Richard F. Russell ★ Robert Ryster ★ J

<u>Thomas Patience's Name Enlarged</u>
(photo by Reba N. Burruss-Barnes, Publicist)

What? A Colored Patience I didn't know anything about? Who could he possibly be?

I knew I must research the military records of this unknown Patience soldier, but with all I was doing at the time, I would have to put him on the "back burner." I would get to him when I could find an opportune time.

A year would pass before that would happen. I was in Fort Wayne, Indiana, to teach composition for a Bridge Program for inner city high school students. It was being held on the Indiana University-Purdue University Fort Wayne campus where Christine Patterson was the Director of the Office of Multicultural Services and Lecturer of Women's Studies and History.

A class field trip was planned at the Allen County Public Library, which at that time housed the second largest genealogical repository in the United States, following only Salt Lake City, Utah. I figured that while

I was there, I should take advantage of the opportunity to research the military records of Pvt. Thomas Patience. What I wanted to learn was where he had been born and at what age had he enlisted in the Union Army. When, where, and why had he joined the 5th MA (Col'd) Cavalry? Would finding such information satisfy my curiosity regarding this heretofore unknown Patience?

After asking the receptionist where the records of the 5th Massachusetts (Col'd) Cavalry were kept, I was directed to an old fashioned wooden cabinet where rolls of microfilm of Civil War records are stored. After locating the 5th Massachusetts (Col'd) Cavalry's, I selected a projection booth where I threaded the microfilm. Then I swiftly scrolled through the alphabetized surnames to "P" and finally reached Pvt. Thomas Patience, Co. B. Then what did my wandering, wondering eyes behold? Twenty-four-year-old Thomas Patience had been born in Chowan County, North Carolina—the very same county as my great grandfather. What astonishing news!!

Pvt. Thomas Patience Was Born in Chowan County, N.C.

Allen County Public Library
Ft. Wayne, IN

Might Thomas and Crowder be brothers, then—both being born in the same county and both having the same unusual surname? My inquiring mind wanted to know, and so in 2003, I commenced on this amazing journey to find the answer to this question: *Does a fraternal relationship exist between Pvt. Crowder Patience of the 103rd PA Volunteers and Pvt. Thomas Patience of the 5th MA (Col'd) Cavalry?*

How could I possibly solve this 154-year-old mystery? Where to begin? A trip to Edenton, N.C., might be the perfect first step. There I shared my quest with a number of citizens. Besides, I researched records at the Shepard-Pruden Library and the Chowan County Courthouse, but to no avail. The surname Pacien, Patience or any similar spelling could not be found.

Another goal had been to discover from which plantation my great grandfather Crowder had absconded. I wanted to include its name under FACTS in my novel, *Created to Be Free,* not yet published. Disappointed, I would come away empty-handed on all counts.

My second visit to Edenton was in 2004 after I had learned of Thomas Patience's existence and after I had obtained a copy of his death certificate. On it no cemetery name had been recorded, only that he had been buried in Chowan County. But where? Not in the Providence African American Cemetery where I looked first. In addition, I was not able to locate funeral records of the long ago deceased undertaker, either.

Providence African American Cemetery
Edenton, N.C.
(photo by Reba N. Burruss-Barnes, Publicist)

Lastly, I was disappointed not to be able to find a tombstone with Thomas Patience's name on it, not even among those at the Warren Grove Baptist Church where he had married his second wife Serena Harris.

Warren Grove Baptist Church
Edenton, N.C.
(photo by Reba N. Burruss Barnes, Publicist)

Once again I would leave Edenton N.C., disappointed. My main goal had not been fulfilled. I had not found the burial site of Pvt. Thomas Patience to ascertain whether or not it has a Union tombstone. After the multiple inquiries with no answers, I began to wonder why Thomas Patience's name seemingly had disappeared from Edenton's Black history, albeit documents exist that substantiate his return in 1867 as well as his death and burial in 1929. As I was taking my leave, I resolved to return someday with this mystery solved.

Fifteen years would pass before its solution was revealed quite unexpectedly through the results of a simple *23andMe* DNA test in 2018. It would introduce me to an Edenton born and reared cousin who possessed genealogical information totally unknown to me and I possessed historical information equally unknown to him.

My questions prior to 2018 had been the following:

1. **Who was Pvt. Thomas Patience who served in the 5th MA (Col'd) Cavalry?**
2. **Who were his people in Edenton, N.C.?**
3. **Where is he buried in Chowan County, N.C.?**
4. **Is his gravesite identified by a Union tombstone?**
5. **If he has descendants, do they know about his Civil War service?**
6. **Are Crowder and Thomas Patience brothers?**

Read on to learn about the astonishing surprises we newly found cousins have encountered.

CHAPTER 7

PVT. THOMAS PATIENCE THE SOLDIER

Thomas Patience's timeline to his first muster-roll on May 31, 1864, began even before he absconded from bondage. Possibly, it had begun the very first time he heard "over the grapevine" that Yankee soldiers were nearby, and that if he could just get to them, he would be free. That "telegraph" was very busy in 1863. Slaves began escaping in droves—running towards freedom.

Pvt. Thomas Patience's Volunteer Enlistment for Three Years

Broadfoot Publishing Company[58]
Researched the National Archives

To read content easily, turn to next page.

VOLUNTEER ENLISTMENT
STATE OF MASSACHUSETTS   CITY OF ROXBURY

"I, <u>Thomas D. Patience</u> was born in <u>Chowan Co.</u> in the state of <u>North Carolina</u> aged <u>Twenty-four years</u> and by occupation a <u>Farmer</u>. Do hereby acknowledge to have volunteered this <u>Thirteenth day</u> of <u>May</u> 18<u>64</u> to serve as a soldier in the Army of the United States of America, for the period of three years, unless sooner discharged by proper authority. Do also agree to accept such bounty, pay, rations, and clothing, as are, or may be established by law for volunteers. And I, <u>Thomas D. Patience</u> do solemnly swear, that I will bear true faith and allegiance to the United States of America, and that I will serve them honestly and faithfully against all their enemies or opposers whomsoever; and that I will observe and obey the orders of the President of the United States, and the orders of the officers appointed over me according to the Rules and Articles of War."

<u>Pvt. Thomas Patience's Volunteer Enlistment for Three Years</u>
National Archives

"I, _Thomas D. Patience_ desiring to VOLUNTEER as a Soldier in the Army of the United States, for the term of THREE YEARS, Do Declare That I am _Twenty-four years_ and_____months of age; that I have never been discharged from the United States service on account of disability or by sentence of a court-martial, or by order before the expiration of a term of enlistment; and I know of no impediment to my serving honestly and faithfully as a soldier for three years.

                        Given at _Boston, Mass_
                        the _thirteenth_ day of _May 1864_

                                   Thomas X Patience"
                                   [_his mark_][59]

Pvt. Thomas D. Patience's Recruit Declaration
May 13, 1864
National Archives

| 5 Col'd Cav. | Mass.

Thomas D. Patience

Appears with rank of *Private* on

Muster and Descriptive Roll of a Detachment of U. S. Vols. forwarded

for the 5 Reg't Mass. Col'd Cavalry. Roll dated Galloup's Island Mass May 31, 1864.

Where born Chowan Co. N.C.

Age 24 y'rs; occupation Farmer

When enlisted May 13, 1864.

Where enlisted Roxbury Mass

For what period enlisted 3 years.

Eyes Black; hair Black

Complexion Black; height 5 ft. 4 in.

When mustered in May 13, 1864.

Where mustered in Galloup's Island Mass

Bounty paid $ 100; due $ 100

Where credited 3 Cong Dist Roxbury Norfolk Co. Mass.

Pvt. Thomas D. Patience's Muster and Descriptive Roll
of a Detachment of U.S. Volunteers
May 31, 1864
(height discrepancies on different documents)
National Archives

To read content easily, turn to next page.

P   **5 Col'd Cav**   **Mass**

Thomas D. Patience

Appears with the rank of *Private.*

Muster and Descriptive Roll of a Detachment of U.S. Vols. forwarded for the 5 Reg't Mass. Col'd Cavalry. Roll dated

Galloups Island, Mass.; May 31, 1864.

Where born *Chowan Co. N.C.*

Age *24 y'rs* occupation *Farmer*

When enlisted *May 13, 1864.*

Where enlisted *Roxbury, Mass.*

For what period enlisted *3 years.*

Eyes *Black ;* Hair *Black*

Complexion *Black;* Height *5 ft. 4 in.*

When mustered in *May 13, 1864.*

Where mustered in *Galloups Island, Mass.*

Pvt. Thomas D. Patience's Muster and Descriptive Roll
of a Detachment of U.S. Volunteers
May 31, 1864

(height discrepancies on different documents)

National Archives

Pvt. Thomas Patience's Co. B Muster-Roll
For May & June 1864
National Archives

Just how long had young Thomas Patience been plotting his escape before he made it happen? Just where, when, and why had he been recruited by the 5th MA (Col'd) Cavalry? Was it because his horsemanship had been skilled enough to satisfy the Union officers?

These particular questions may forever remain unanswered. What happened, however, to the recruits who arrived at Gallapos Island, Massachusetts, eager to become United States cavalrymen, is detailed in Steven LaBarre's *The Fifth Massachusetts Colored Cavalry in the Civil War*[60] and John Wright Warner Jr.'s *Crossed Sabres*.[61]

In February 1863 after receiving permission from the Secretary of War, Edwin M. Stanton, the abolitionist Massachusetts Governor, John Albion Andrew, formed two regiments of Colored men—the 54th and 55th MA Infantry. With both regiments having filled quickly, the Governor proposed next the formation of a cavalry unit. He would recruit fro near and far to fill it. For instance, Charles Douglass[62], son of orator Frederick Douglass, was from nearby West Roxbury, Mass., while two seamen were from as far away as Hawaii. [63]

Companies formed were A-M, excluding "J" since the letters "J" and "I" might get confused by quill-pen and ink record keepers. The cavalry's companies filled rapidly and were trained on horseback. Unexpectedly, though, three months later they would be ordered to dismount and immediately converted from cavalrymen bearing sabers into infantrymen bearing muskets.[64]

Then to add more insult to its disappointment and disillusionment, the regiment was assigned to the Point Lookout Prison in Maryland on the Chesapeake Bay. There those Black soldiers, many having been former slaves, were ordered to guard white prisoners of war, many having been slave owners.

Both captives and captors detested the environment as much as they detested each other. The hatred emanating from the two groups towards each other must have seemed nearly palpable.

During its twenty-two months of existence, Point Lookout confined 52,264 Confederate soldiers and civilians. Approximately 3,000 prisoners died due to such abhorrent conditions as inadequate shelter, medical care, food supplies, and fuel, as well as extremes in temperatures during changing seasons. [65]

> **P.** | 5 Col'd Cav. | **Mass.**
>
> Thomas Patience,
>
> Pvt., Co. B, 5 Reg't Mass. Col'd Cavalry.
>
> Appears on
>
> Company Muster Roll
>
> for *Sept. & Oct.*, 1864.
>
> Present or absent... — *Present*
>
> Stoppage, $............ 100 for ....
>
> Due Gov't, $............ 100 for ....
>
> Valuation of horse, $............ 100
>
> Valuation of horse equipments, $............ 100
>
> Remarks: *Free on or before Apr. 19/61.*
>
> *Due U.S. Bounty $25.00*

<u>Pvt. Thomas Patience's Co. B Muster Roll</u>
for Sept. & Oct. 1864
Remarks: *Free on or before Apr. 19/61*[66]

Due U.S. Bounty $25.00

National Archives

```
P.  |  5 Col'd Cav.  | Mass.

Thomas Patience,

Pvt., Co. B, 5 Reg't Mass. Col'd Cavalry.

Appears on

Company Muster Roll

for Nov. & Dec., 1864.

Present or absent... Present.
```

Pvt. Thomas Patience's Co. B Muster Roll
for Nov. & Dec. 1864
National Archives

The tedium of guarding the Confederate prisoners was broken for the 5th MA (Col'd) Cavalry when they celebrated the new National holiday set by President Abraham Lincoln in 1864 for the last Thursday of November. He designated it to be a day of thanksgiving. It would be the first holiday the regiment had celebrated since its formation. Each company was treated to a sumptuous Thanksgiving Day turkey dinner that was accompanied by much joviality.

"The unit gathered together as a family within their camp at Point Lookout for a day of festivities, comradeship, and a meal fit for a king."[67]

Pvt. Thomas Patience's Co. B Muster Roll
For March & April 1865
National Archives

At the end of March 1865, duty at Point Lookout, Maryland, ended for the 5th MA. Under the command of Colonel Charles F. Adams Jr., great-grandson of President John Adams and grandson of President John Quincy Adams, it was ordered to Petersburg, Va. Following the victory there, it was remounted on April 2, 1865. On the next morning, the single Black cavalry raised in the North would become the first Black cavalry to victoriously enter Richmond.[68]

Jubilant freed slaves streaming into the city streets could not believe what their astonished eyes were beholding—lines of horses with hundreds of blue uniformed Black soldiers astride them,[69] triumphantly entering the capitol the defeated Confederates had ignited and abandoned just hours before.[70]

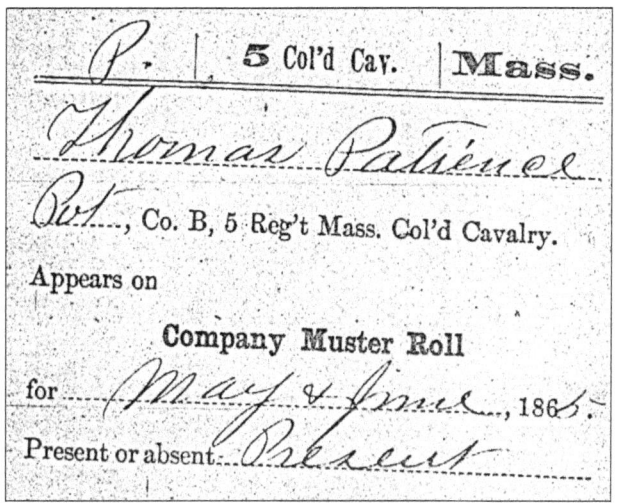

Pvt. Thomas Patience's Co. B Muster Roll May & June 1865

National Archives

The Confederate surrender took place on April 9, 1865, at Appomattox Court House, Virginia. The war-weary soldiers at last were going home. Not the 5th Massachusetts (Col'd) Cavalry, though. It had not yet fulfilled its three-year commitment. Since many disgruntled Confederates were causing problems at the Mexican border, military opinion was who better to send to Brazos, Texas,[71] than the 5th? Another stinging insult to the regiment.

Again it was being ordered to a duty where conditions would be so abhorrent that the soldiers became ill quickly, resulting in frequent hospital stays and numerous deaths.[72] Years later when applying for an invalid pension, the reasons veteran Thomas Patience would offer were weakened eyes and other ailments that had hospitalized him at Brazos, Texas.

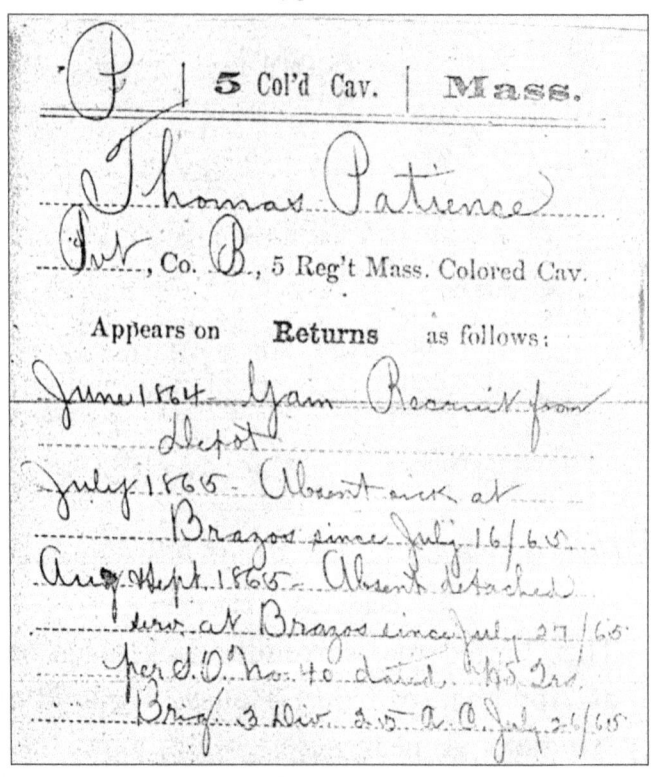

Pvt. Thomas Patience on Co. B Returns

July 1865- Absent sick at Brazos since July 16/65

Aug. & Sept. 1865- Absent detached serv.

at Brazos since July 27/65

per G.O. No. 40 dated ?

Brig. 3 Div. 25 C C July 26/65

National Archives

| P | 5 Col'd Cav. | **Mass.** |

Thomas Patience

Pvt., Co. B, 5 Reg't Mass. Col'd Cavalry.

Appears on **Co. Muster-out Roll**, dated
Clarkesville, Tex., Oct. 31, 1865.

Muster-out to date Oct. 31, 1865.

Last paid to Dec. 31, 1864.

Clothing account:

Last settled............, 186 ; drawn since $........100

Due soldier $............100; due U. S. $ 21 41/100

Am't for cloth'g in kind or money adv'd $........100

Due U. S. for arms, equipments, &c., $ 11 00/100

Bounty paid $ 25 00/100; due $ 75 00/100

Remarks:................................

Pvt. Thomas Patience's Muster-Out Roll

Clarkesville, Texas
October 31, 1865

National Archives

Pvt. Thomas Patience was mustered-out in Clarkesville, Texas, on October 31, 1865. After paying his debt with the bounty[73] promised at his enlistment, he received $11.00 as his final pay.

Needless to say, when I was reading Pvt. Thomas Patience's records for the very first time, I became quite excited; so much so, I emitted an audible exclamation in that very quiet Indiana library. A 154-year-old mystery was unfolding before my very eyes!

Again the same unanswered questions were bombarding my mind. Are Crowder and Thomas brothers? Where is Thomas Patience buried? Does a Union tombstone mark his gravesite like the one marking Crowder Patience's in the West Pittston Cemetery in Pennsylvania?

Has Thomas Patience's story been passed to successive generations or might it have been forgotten through the years? Crowder Patience's story has been cherished by his descendants. For instance, in 2016 a g-g-g-great grandson, Matthew Allen Patience,[74] at age eight became the youngest to share an ancestor's story during the monthly first Saturday Descendants' Hour held at the African American Civil War Museum in Washington, D.C.

<u>Youngest Presenter Matthew Allen Patience With</u>
<u>Family</u>
<u>Parents</u>: Karen and Jason
<u>L-R</u>: Brothers Mason and Matthew
2016
(photo by Reba N. Burruss-Barnes)

African American Civil War Museum Sign-In Sheet

Matthew Patience- Youngest Speaker

Also signing were Brother Mason and Grandmother Rosalind

August 6, 2016

(photo by Reba N. Burruss Barnes)

CHAPTER 8
CONFUSING SURNAME SPELLINGS

The unusual surname of Crowder and Thomas had several different spellings. On documents of both, it has been spelled as "Pashions," "Pacient," "Patient," and "Pations," but only on Crowder's is "Pacien" found. Such differences are seen not only on Thomas' pension applications, but also on accompanying affidavits from witnesses who knew him well.

Surname Spelled "Pashions/Patience"

(his father's surname?)

National Archives

To read content easily, turn to next page.

GENERAL AFFIDAVIT

State of _N. Carolina_, County of _Chowan_

In the matter *of _Tho^s Pashions_*

"On this _15_ day of _June_ A.D. _1900_, personally appeared before me, _Clerk Superior Court_ in and for the aforesaid County, duly authorized to administer oaths _Tho^s Pashions_ aged _60_ years, a resident near _Clum_ in the County of _Chowan_ and State of _N.C._ whose Post-Office is _Clum, N.C._ is well known to me to be reputable and entitled to credit and who, being duly sworn, declares in relation to aforesaid case as follows:

That he enlisted under the name of Thos Patience or Pashions. That he is not familiar with the spelling of his name but it was the surname of his father.

That in making affidavits the spelling of his name may be different in different affidavits but it was no fault of his. He believes the correct spelling is Thos Pashions."

(Return to Joseph H. Hunter . Attorney. Washington, D.C.)

Surname Spelled "Pashions/Patience"

(his father's surname?)

National Archives

CHAPTER 9

THE BROTHER WHO RETURNED HOME

Upon discovering that Thomas Patience had been born in the same county in North Carolina as my great grandfather, I knew I must find all I could about the Patience soldier who had served in the 5th MA (Col'd) Cavalry. So I wrote to Broadfoot Publishing Company in Wilmington, N.C., to order copies of Thomas' military and invalid pension[75] documents. Every Civil War veteran did not receive a pension, but, fortunately, Thomas Patience had. Consequently, I was able to glean a great deal of information about him from the affidavits presented on his behalf by neighbors and friends who had known him both before and after the Civil War.

From his military records I learned that after the war ended, he was mustered out of the Union Army in Texas. He would have to travel to Boston for his discharge and final pay because in order to receive any bounties promised at enlistment, soldiers had to return to the place of their mustering-in. So for the North Carolinian Thomas Patience, that was Massachusetts.

While serving in the 5th MA (Col'd) Cavalry, he had caught glimpses of different locales, including Norfolk, Virginia; Baltimore, Maryland; Boston, Massachusetts; Washington, D.C.; New Orleans, Louisiana; New York City, New York; and Philadelphia,

Pennsylvania. As he was being transported north on a steam boat back to Boston, might remembrances of such urban lifestyles have sparked the young man to ponder future plans for his life? The Yankees had won the war and now freedom was his to claim. Finally, he could, and would, make choices concerning his own destiny.

He was well aware that returning home could mean laboring in fields again—this time for wages, though. He might choose someday to purchase some acreage of his very own. He might even choose to marry and to rear a family. So perhaps with such positive thoughts in mind, Thomas Patience chose to return to Edenton, N.C., where he arrived in the fall of 1867.

What kind of reception did Thomas receive from his family and neighbors who may not have expected ever to see him again? I can only imagine their jubilation.

Affidavits reveal that, indeed, he did return to laboring in the fields. He did marry and rear four children. Later, his first son purchased land in Edenton, property still possessed by his descendants to this day.

CHAPTER 10

THOMAS PATIENCE THE CITIZEN

Where would Thomas Patience live after his return to Edenton? When he had left in 1863, his family was enslaved, but when he returned in 1867, they were free. One witness to Thomas' return from war was his neighbor, Walter W. Harris.

W. W. Harris Witnessed Thomas Patience's Return Home
1867

AFFIDAVIT

State of <u>North Carolina</u>   County of <u>Chowan</u>

" In claim <u>Thomas Patience</u> of <u>Edenton, Chowan, NC</u> of Co. <u>B</u> of the <u>5</u>th Regt. of <u>Mass US C Cal</u> personally appeared before the undersigned duly authorized to administer oaths within and for the County and State aforesaid <u>W. W. Harris</u> age <u>54</u> years whose P.O. is <u>Edenton</u>, County of <u>Chowan, State NC , Route No 1. Box 14</u> whom I certify to be credible, who being duly sworn states in relation to said claim as follows, to wit:

That he is well acquainted with the claimant Thomas Patience before the Civil War. When he came home from the war in 1867 and stopped at my father's house and I know that it was the same Thomas Patience that I knew when I was a boy. Don't know what Co. and Reg. he was in, but he had all the equipment used, also uniform."

<u>W. W. Harris Witnessed Thomas Patience's Return Home</u>

1867

National Archives

Tracking down Thomas Patience's whereabouts after his return to Edenton has not been an easy task. For one reason, in later years when he applied for an invalid pension, he had used other Post Office addresses: Myra and Clum, North Carolina. Perhaps they were not towns, I have been told, but most likely they were just mail stations located a few miles out of the town of Edenton.

A second difficulty I encountered is that in spite of Walter W. Harris' attesting to having spoken with the returning soldier in 1867, three years later Thomas Patience was not counted for the 1870 census. Where was he, when for the first time he would have been counted as a whole person and not a mere 3/5?[76] Furthermore, why was he not be counted for the 1880 and 1900 censuses, either? As for the 1890 census, unfortunately, most of it was destroyed by a fire in Washington, D.C.

Thomas Patience's whereabouts during the 1900 census count was particularly puzzling since in 1907 he applied for an invalid pension. He had developed severe rheumatism, was almost blind and prone to epilepsy. Note his answer to question 10, stating that he had lived in Chowan County since returning home from the war:

Department of the Interior

BUREAU OF PENSIONS

Mr. Thomas Patience   Edenton, North Carolina

1. When were you born? Answer. *1839.*
2. Where were you born? Answer. *Chowan County.*
3. When did you enlist? Answer. *1863.*
4. Where did you enlist? Answer. *Norfolk, Va.*
. Where had you lived before you enlisted? Answer *In Chowan Co., N.C.*
6. What was your post-office address at enlistment? Answer. *Edenton, N.C.*
7. What was your occupation at enlistment? Answer. *Slave Laborer.*
8. When were you discharged? Answer. *About 1867.*
9. Where were you discharged? Answer. *Was taken from Brazwell, Texas, to Boston.*
10. Where have you lived since discharge? Give dates as nearly as possible, of any changes of residence.
    Answer. *Have lived in Chowan County since I came out of the Army.*
11. What is your present occupation? Answer. *Farm Laborer.*
12. What is your height? Answer. *5 feet 4 inches.*
    Your weight? *132*
    The color of your eyes? *Black.* The color of your hair? *Black.* Your complexion? *Black.*
    Are there any permanent marks or scars on your person? If so, describe them. *None.*
13. What is your full name   *Thomas X Patience*

     Witnesses: Nov 2, 1907
     W. R. Brothers
     Lee Chappell

National Archives

On an accompanying affidavit, neighbor John Hathaway attested to Thomas Patience's veracity when applying for an invalid pension:

"That he knew the claimant well before the Civil War—both of them worked close together—knew that he enlisted in the army but not in the same regiment.

I was in the infantry and he in the cavalry. After the war was over he came home and we worked on adjoining farms, saw him every week and we used to talk about the times we had while in the service. I further certify that this claimant is correct name. Thomas Patience."

Only for the 1910 census was Thomas Patience counted as a resident of Edenton. He was living on Cowpen Neck Road with his wife, Serena [nee Harris], whom he married in 1895 at the Warren Grove Baptist Church.[77]

Their neighbors in 1910 had included Michael and Cornelia Lawrence, who ten years later would be counted in the 1920 census. Neither Thomas nor Serena Patience would be, though. Since he did not pass away until 1929, why had Thomas Patience not been counted for the 1920 census?

Verse II

"Stony the road we trod, bitter the chastening rod
Felt in the days when hope unborn had died.
Yet with a steady beat, have not our weary feet
Come to the place for which our people sighed.

We have come over a way that with tears have been watered.
We have come treading our path through the blood of the slaughtered.
Out from the gloomy past, till now we stand at last
Where the bright gleam of our bright star is cast."

       James Weldon Johnson
         (1871-1938)

CHAPTER 11

PENSION APPLICATONS & AFFIDAVITS

Regardless of race, an incentive for enlisting in the Union Army was the promise of a pension if the soldier were injured. The payment amount would depend on the soldier's rank and the extent of his injuries. In 1862 during the war, the pension system was granting $8.00 per month to a "totally disabled" private.[78]

As the war escalated and the need for manpower increased, the pension became a valuable tool for attracting new recruits. Following the war, however, pensions were difficult to secure due to strict criteria, such as proof that a veteran's disabilities were due to his war experiences, and not to "vicious living."

In addition, lawyers needed to be hired for submitting veterans' information to Washington, D.C. Black veterans, especially, were at a decided disadvantage because many did not have enough money to hire a lawyer.[79] Thomas Patience was fortunate enough to be able to hire Joseph Hunter, named on the first pension application dated August 6, 1892. Later, Edward Gaddis was Thomas' second lawyer, whose fee in 1908 was $70.00.

ACT OF JUNE 27, 1890.

Declaration for Original Pension

See file

NOTICE.—This can be executed before a Notary Public, Justice of the Peace, or a Court of Record, or any officer duly qualified to administer oaths.

State of _N. Carolina_, County of _Chowan_, ss:

ON THIS _6th_ day of _August_, A. D. one thousand eight hundred and ninety-_two_, personally appeared before me a _Clerk of Superior Court_, within and for the county and State aforesaid _Thomas Pashions_, aged _54_ years, a resident of _Myra_, County of _Chowan_, State of _N. C._, who, being duly sworn according to law, declares that he is the identical _Thos Pashions_ who was ENROLLED at _Norfolk_ sometime day of _____ 186_2_, in Company _C_ of the _5th_ Regiment of _Mass Cav_ Vols., in the War of the Rebellion and served at least ninety days, and was honorably DISCHARGED at _Boston Mass._ during _later Fall_ of 186_5_.

That he is _____ unable to earn a support by manual labor by reason of _disease of Eyes and rheumatism in loins hips_.

That said disabilities are not due to his vicious habits, and are to the best of his knowledge and belief permanent.

That he has _never_ applied for pension under application No. _____. That he is a pensioner under Certificate No. _____

That he has _not_ been employed in the military or naval service otherwise than as stated above

and when ordered for examination desires to be ordered before the Board of Surgeons at _E. City_, County of _Pasquotank_, State of _N.C._

That he makes this declaration for the purpose of being placed on the pension roll of the United States, under act of Congress approved June 27, 1890. He hereby appoints,

JOSEPH H. HUNTER, of Washington, D. C.,

his true and lawful attorney to prosecute his claim. That he hereby agrees to allow his said attorney a fee of $10 when the claim is allowed. That his Post Office address is _Myra_, County of _Chowan_, State of _N C_.

James C Wilson   Tom X Pations
Squire new Bern   Signature of claimant.

Thos Pashions First Invalid Pension Application
a.k.a Tom X Pations
August 6, 1892
(Company C is incorrect.)

National Archives

Thomas Patience's personal struggles to obtain an invalid pension illustrate the kinds of difficulties Civil War veterans had to overcome. When applying for the first time in 1892 due to his declining health, Thomas Patience had submitted the following complaints:

"I had severe sore eyes during the war while in Texas. Eyesight has been bad since. Has had the rheumatism for 2 or 3 years. Last winter was confined to the house for over two months. Part of the time in bed. Can only do light work now. Had the rheumatism in hips, knees, and left shoulder."

According to the following medical assessments, though, neither Thomas's eye problems nor his rheumatism were severe enough to warrant his receiving the coveted government invalid pension:

"No disease apparent of the eyes, vision normal for his age except he is nearsighted. No rating.

Evidence of rheumatism is showed by crepitation[80] in both shoulder joints, tenderness and slight loss of motion in right shoulder joint, etc.

Entitled to a Eight Eighteenth rating.[81] No other disability found to exist."

Thomas Patience would apply a second time on August 4, 1898, again complaining of sore eyes due to his service with his regiment in Texas. An accompanying report from the Clerk of the Superior Court of the State of North Carolina, County of Chowan, stated:

"That he has had no treatment by physicians since Aug. 10, 1892 for his eyes and rheumatism. He was stricken by epilepsy two summers ago and had physicians to attend him for that. He had Dr. Thomas Warren to treat his eyes and rheumatism directly after the war but Warren has been dead many years. He also got some medicine several years ago from Dr. W. J. Leary. Leary is also dead.

So that it is impossible for him to produce any medical evidence of disabilities up to year 1892 and one since that time because he has not had any treatment since that time except what he has done for himself. He in fact believes he receives more relief for his rheumatism from his home treatment than from scientific treatment and therefore has never relied very much upon physicians.

He asks that the affidavits of Major Bonn and J. R. Davis his neighbors be taken in lieu of medical evidence."

National Archives

GENERAL AFFIDAVIT.

State of **N Carolina**, County of **Chowan**, ss:

In the matter of **Thos. Pashions**
                      Claimant's name.

ON THIS **4** day of **Aug.**, A. D. 189**8**, personally appeared before me, a **Clerk Supr. Court** in and for the aforesaid County, duly authorized to administer oaths, **Major Bonn** aged **57** years, a resident of **near Edenton** in the County of **Chowan** and State of **N Carolina** whose Post-Office address is **Edenton, N.C.**, **J.R. Davis** aged **49** years, a resident of **near Edenton** in the County of **Chowan** and State of **N.C.** whose Post-Office address is **Edenton, N.C.** well known to me to be reputable and entitled to credit, and who, being duly sworn, declares in relation to aforesaid case as follows:

That they have personal acquaintance with said Thomas Pashion & know him to suffer very greatly on account of Rheumatism & distase of eyes. They have worked in the field with him & have seen him on an average at least once a month during the last past 25 years & know of their own personal knowledge that he is not able to work but a very small part of his time & that when he does try to work he cannot do more than 1/3 of a good man's work — That being a Laborer his services are worth very little when he can work because he cannot see well & will not do to trust to do certain form work — They know that said disabilities are not the result of vicious habits — That to their certain knowledge said Pashion has been disabled to the extent of 2/3 by his said disabilities from Aug 10th 1892 to July 27th 1898 —

GENERAL AFFIDAVIT

State of <u>N. Carolina</u>, County of <u>Chowan</u>,

In the matter of <u>Thos Pashions</u>

ON THIS <u>4</u> day of <u>Aug</u>, A.D. 189<u>8</u>, *personally appeared before me, a* <u>Clerk Superior Court</u> *in and for the aforesaid County, duly authorized to administer oaths,* <u>Major Bonn</u> *aged* <u>57</u> *years, a resident of near Edenton in the County of* <u>Chowan</u> *and State of* <u>N. Carolina</u> *whose Post-Office address is* <u>Edenton, N.C.</u> *and* <u>J. R. Davis</u> *aged* <u>49</u> *years, …declares:*

"That they have personal acquaintance with said Thomas Pashions and know him to suffer very greatly on account of Rheumatism and disease of eyes. They have worked in the field with him and have seen him on an average of at least once a month during the last 25 years and know of their own personal knowledge that he is not able to work for a very small part of his time and that when he does try to work he cannot do more than 1/3 of a good man's work. That being a laborer his services are worth very little when he can work because he cannot see well and will not do too much to do certain farm work. They know that said disabilities are not the result of vicious habits. That to their certain knowledge said Pashions has been disabled to the extent of 2/3 by his said disabilities from August 10, 1892 to July 27, 1898."

<u>Major Bonn and John R. Davis' Affidavit in 1898</u>

Even with such sworn affidavits, Thomas Patience's application for an invalid pension was rejected. The medical examiner accessed, *"no disease of eyes. 18/20 in either eye."* As for the rheumatism, Thomas' rating this time was 12/18,[82] The report concluded: *"no evidence of vicious habits and no other disability found."*

Years passed while Thomas Patience's health steadily declined. New applications were filed with witnesses again attesting that his disabilities did not have anything to do with *"vicious living."* Such witnesses included neighbors and friends: Major Bonn, William Riley Brothers, Lee Chappell, John Davis, Walter W. Harris, L. L. Howell, John Hathaway, W. P. Simpson, J. W. Spruill, and John Standing.

After applying again in 1906, Thomas Patience finally was deemed eligible for an invalid pension. In September of 1907 a new law was passed to include "old age" as a disability.[83] At age 68 he began receiving $12.00 per month.

"Declaration filed September 21, 1906, alleges permanent disability, not due to vicious habits, from Epilepsy, defective sight, and rheumatism."

Act of February 6, 1907.

Declaration for Pension.

The Pension Certificate SHOULD NOT Be Forwarded With the Application.

State of North Carolina
County of Chowan } ss.

On this 4 day of March, A. D. one thousand nine hundred and Seven, personally appeared before me, a Notary Public within and for the county and State aforesaid Thomas Patience, who, being duly sworn according to law, declares that he is 68 YEARS OF AGE, and resident of near Edenton county of Chowan, State of NC; and that he is the identical person who was ENROLLED at Norfolk Va under the name of Thomas Patience, on the ___ day of April, 1864 as a private, in Co B 5th Mass cal vol cav (Here state rank, and company and regiment in the Army, or vessels if in the Navy.)

in the service of the United States, in the Civil War, war, and was HONORABLY DISCHARGED at Boston Mass, on the ___ day of September, 1866. That he also served _____

That he has not been employed in the military or naval service of the United States except as stated above. That his personal description at enlistment was as follows: Height, 5 feet 7 inches; complexion, Dark; color of eyes, Black; color of hair, Black; that his occupation was farm hand; that he was born November, 1838 at Weale farm near Edenton NC

That his several places of residence since leaving the service have been as follows: in Chowan county, NC no where else

That he is not a pensioner by Certificate No. _____, at $ ___ per month. That he has _____ heretofore applied for pension, Claim No. 1126174

That he makes this declaration for the purpose of being placed on the pension roll of the United States under the provisions of the act of February 6, 1907, and any amendments thereof.

He hereby appoints, with full power of substitution, **EDGAR T. GADDIS**, of Washington, D. C., his successors or legal representatives, his true and lawful attorney to prosecute his claim under said law; and he requests and directs that he be allowed and paid, upon the issuance of a certificate, or thereafter, such fee or compensation as may be hereafter provided by law or ruling.

That his post-office address is Edenton county of Chowan State of NC

Thomas Patience (Claimant's signature in full)

Attest: (1) W. R. Brothers
(2) A. A. Johnston

Also personally appeared W R Brothers, residing in Edenton NC and A A Johnson, residing in Edenton NC, persons whom I certify to be respectable and entitled to credit, and who, being by me duly sworn, say that they were present and saw Thomas Patience, the claimant, sign his name (or make his mark) to the foregoing declaration; that they have every reason to believe, from the appearance of the claimant and their acquaintance with him of One year and One years, respectively, that he is the identical person he represents himself to be, and that they have no interest in the prosecution of this claim.

W. R. Brothers
A. A. Johnston
(Signatures of witnesses.)

Subscribed and sworn to before me this 4 day of March, A. D. 1907.

Thomas Patience's Pension Application in 1907

Under Act of February 6, 1907

(questionable birth date)

National Archives

To read content easily, turn to next page.

DECLARATION FOR PENSION

State of North Carolina County of Chowan

"On this <u>4</u> day of <u>March</u>, A.D. one thousand nine hundred and <u>Seven</u> personally appeared before me, a <u>Notary Republic</u> within and for the county and state aforesaid <u>Thomas Patience</u>, who, being duly sworn according to law, declares that he is <u>68</u> years of age, and resident <u>near Edenton</u> county of <u>Chowan,</u> State of <u>N.C.</u> and he is the identical person who was enrolled at <u>Norfolk, Va.</u> under the name of Thomas Patience, on the --- day of <u>April, 1864</u> as a <u>private</u>, in <u>Co B 5th Mass Col. Vol Cav</u> in the service of the United States, in the <u>Civil War</u>, and was honorably discharged in <u>Boston, Mass.</u>, on the ---day of <u>September, 1866.</u>

That he has <u>not</u> been employed in the military or naval service in the United States except as stated above.

That his personal description at enlistment was as follows: Height <u>5</u> feet <u>7</u> inches; complexion, <u>Dark</u>; color of eyes, <u>Black</u>; color of hair, <u>Black</u>; that his occupation was <u>farm hand</u>; that he was born <u>November, 1838</u> at <u>Breole farm near Edenton, N.C.</u>

That his several places of residence since leaving the service have been as follows: <u>in Chowan County N.C. no where else.</u>"

<u>*Thomas Patience's Pension Application in 1907*</u>
Under Act of February 6, 1907
(questionable birth date)

National Archives

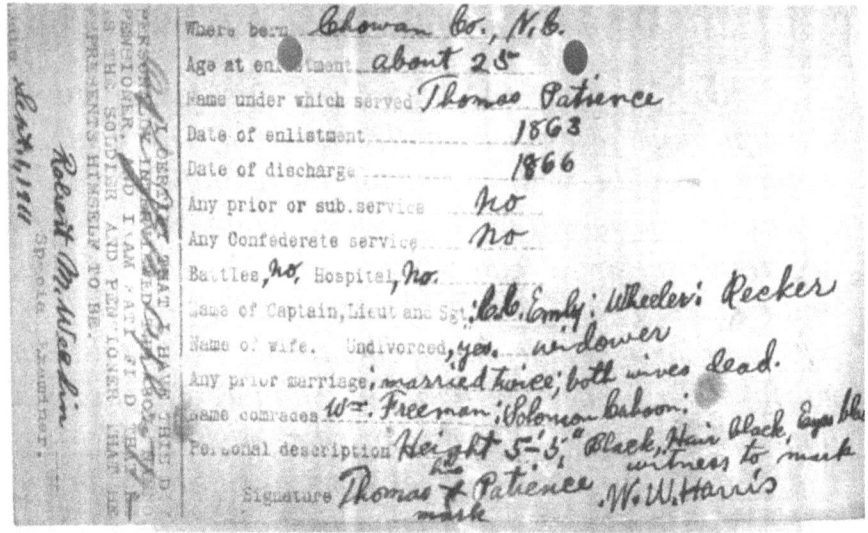

W. W. Harris Witnessed Thomas Patience's Mark
1911
National Archives

Robert M. Weelin, Special Examiner, signed on September 1, 1911:

"I certify that I have personally interviewed the above named pensioner, and I am satisfied that he is the soldier and pensioner that he represents himself to be."

Once again, the Civil War veteran Thomas Patience was being questioned about his identity, even though he and his witnesses provided the same answers each time.

CHAPTER 12

REVELATIONS FOUND ON PENSION APPLICATIONS

A Civil War invalid pension application oftentimes reveals information of personal interest to veterans' descendants, such as their height and weight, even though such information can vary on different documents. Skin, eye and hair color also might be recorded.

From pension applications, descendants might discover mutual familial characteristics. For instance, one of Thomas Patience's applications recorded his physical description as being "a thin dark-complexioned white-haired old man." Such characteristics fit my great grandfather Crowder Patience[84] "to a T," since he, too, was a thin, dark-complexioned, white-haired old man.

If their white hair had been premature, I have no way of knowing. I do know, however, that premature white hair is prevalent in my extended family as is seen in these four generations: my great-aunt Lillie, my father, my son, and me. The same goes for some of my Lawrence cousins.

Also, pension applications might reveal the general health of the veteran. Despite disabilities incurred during his military service when he was young, Thomas Patience would live to be an old man. Although his exact age is not known,[85] he was *circa* 93-years-old when he died in 1929.[86] For many years, he had suffered from rheumatism [arthritis], blaming it on the war, but perhaps not necessarily. From pension applications, descendants might learn of health issues that seem to "run in the family," such as near-sightedness and rheumatism.

Crowder Patience lived a long life, too, passing away suddenly at the age of eight-three from the deadly grippe [influenza] which today is preventable. Consider his daughter Lillian. She lived almost to her 103rd birthday. During her lifetime she had never been seriously ill, even though she had hypertension [high blood pressure] for which she faithfully took her prescribed medicine. Osteoarthritis [rheumatism] had been her only complaint, resulting in reliance on a cane.

Lastly, information found on pension applications can also be of importance to historians. Thomas Patience would identify the farm on which he was born. When I attempted to interpret its name on the document, the 19th century script was illegible to me. All I could discern was a name beginning with a "B," followed by a few letters.

Because the name of the farm was not decipherable to me, I mailed a copy of the document to my friend Rosalie Boyd Miller, the librarian at the Shephard-Pruden Library in Edenton. Unfortunately, she was not able to decipher the name, either. So determined another trip to Edenton was necessary

An opportunity to visit Edenton again came in August 2004 when Rosalie Boyd Miller arranged a speaking engagement for me at the Kadesh A. M. E. Zion Church.[87] The following day I carried my document to the Chowan County Courthouse to see if anyone there might be able to decipher the farm's name. I felt strongly that if Thomas Patience had been born there, then Crowder Patience might have been, too. At first, I was being disappointed again because the name of the farm was undecipherable to the library personnel, too, but a pleasant surprise was in store for me.

For soon afterwards, one of young women helping me with the research would become very excited upon seeing the signature of her great-great grandfather on the document. He was William Riley Brothers who had signed "W. R. Brothers." Piqued with interest now, she suggested we examine Edenton deed books from 1750-1850 to search for a four or five lettered name beginning with "B." We were able to find it quite easily. It was "Briols" which had been misspelled as "Breoles" on Thomas Patience's pension application.

The deed was that of a Francois Briols from Guadaloupe, who had moved to the United States with the hope of making a fortune, possibly by growing rice like some other West Indian planters had. The plantation's history goes back to 1716 when the original owners were John and Ann Jones.[88] The property had four other owners prior to 1795, when a refugee from Guadaloupe, Mll. Constance de Calmetz, purchased it the year before her wedding to Jean Francois Jably de Briols.

Even though the Frenchman Francois Briols returned permanently to Guadaloupe in 1803, something French would stay behind in Edenton—the Briols name. After being sold to John Coffield, the property has changed owners several times with the name remaining.

The original Briols farmhouse still sits on the road formerly known as Briols, too, but presently called Brayhall. For verification, both names can be found on old maps at the Chowan County Courthouse in Edenton.

Chowan County Courthouse [89]

Edenton, N.C.

CHAPTER 13

THOMAS PATIENCE'S PENSION INCREASES

The invalid pension system was changed in 1907 to include any veteran who had survived to the age of seventy. Then, because of that "old age" disability, every veteran would receive a pension for the rest of his life.

Thomas Patience's First Pension Payment
Under Act of February 6, 1907
$12.00 per month
September 1, 1906

Act of June 27, 1890
as amended by the Act of May 9, 1900

INVALID PENSION

Claimant,   **Thomas Patience**

P.O., <u>Edenton</u>	*Rank*, <u>Private</u>
County, <u>Chowan</u>	*Company*, <u>B</u>
State, <u>North Carolina</u> (Col'd)	*Regiment*, <u>5th Mass Vol. Cav</u>

Rate, $12.— *per month, commencing* <u>September 21,</u> 1906.

End pension <u>March 10, 1907</u> by reason of allowance at equal rate under Act of February 6, 1907.

Pensioned for <u>total</u> *inability to earn a support by manual labor.*

RECOGNIZED ATTORNEY

Name <u>Edgar ? Gaddis</u>	*Fee,* <u>$70.⁰⁰</u>
P.O. <u>Washington, D.C.</u>	<u>Agent to pay.</u>

APPROVALS

...

<u>Thomas Patience's First Pension Payment</u>
Under Act of February 6, 1907

$12.00 per month

(commencing September 21, 1906)

AFFIDAVIT

State of North Carolina County of Chowan ss:
In claim No. 1126199 of Thomas Patience
of Co. B of the 5th Mass C.C. Regt. of .... Vols. Personally appeared before the undersigned duly authorized to administer oaths within and for the County and State aforesaid, John Standing about age 70 years, whose P.O. is Edenton County of Chowan State North Carolina whom I certify to be credible, who being duly sworn, states in relation to said claim as follows, to wit:

That I have known the claimant Thomas Patience from boyhood raised & worked on same farm — were slaves to gather. I was carried up the country at Hillsboro, N.C. left him home after the war was over I came back home, he came home also, he told me he had been in the army. We then worked close together ever since he is the same Thomas Patience as I knew him before the war.

And affiant further states that he has no interest in this claim.

W. R. Bythew
Lee Chappell
John X Standing (his mark)

Sworn to and subscribed before me on the 5 day of Oct., 1907, and I hereby certify that the contents of this affidavit were fully made known to the affiant before signing and I have no interest in this claim or its prosecution.

K. R. Pendleton
Notary Public

John Standing's Affidavit For Thomas Patience's Identity

1907

National Archives

State of <u>North Carolina</u>   County of <u>Chowan</u>

"*In claim No. <u>1126179</u> of <u>Thomas Patience</u> of Co. B of the 5th Mass CC Regt. of……. Vols. Personally appeared before the undersigned duly authorized to administer oaths within and for the County and State aforesaid <u>John Standing</u> about age <u>70</u> years whose P.O. is <u>Edenton</u> County of <u>Chowan</u> State <u>North Carolina</u> whom I certify to be credible, who being duly sworn states in relation to said claim as follows, to wit:*

That I have known the claimant Thomas Patience from boyhood, raised and worked on same farm, were slaves together.

I was carried up the country at Hillsboro, NC. left him home. After the war was over I came back home, he came home also, he told me he had been in the army. We then worked close together ever since. He is the same Thomas Patience as I knew him before the war."

<u>John Standing's Affidavit For Thomas Patience's Identity</u>

1907

National Archives

Thomas Patience's Pension Increase in 1910
Under Act of February 6, 1907
$15.00 per Month
(various possible birth years) [90]

National Archives

To read content easily, turn to next page.

Claimant, Thomas Patience

P.O., Edenton *Rank,* Private

County, Chowan *Company,* B

State, North Carolina *Regiment,* 5 Massachusetts Vol Cav (Col'd)

Rate, $15 per month, commencing October 21, 1910

APPROVAL

Submitted for Ad., Oct. 27, 1910, Geo W. Paschal, Examiner

Approved for Increase.

Age over 70

Rate $15. Per Month

...

PRESENT CLAIM, ACT OF FEBRUARY 6, 1907

Declaration filed October 21, 1910.

Date of birth alleged, December 1836; Nov. 1838; also 1839.

Age shown by evidence 70 years.

Claimant does **not** *write.*

J.H. Small

, M.C.

<u>Thomas Patience's Pension Increase in 1910</u>
Under Act of February 6, 1907
$15.00 per Month
(various possible birth years)

National Archives

Oftentimes information found on pension applications was not accurate, or, at best, dubious. Such an example is found with the different birthdates recorded for Thomas Patience. On his death certificate he was recorded as 93-years-old. Had he been born in 1836?

His pension application in 1910, however, lists three alleged birth years, making the exact age at death unknown. The following letter in 1914 contains his own dictated words, claiming Christmas day [91] as his birthday.

Edenton, N.C.   Oct. 13, 1914
Commissioner of Pensions
Washington, D.C.
"Sir:
Certificate No. 1140754 under Act of February 6th 1907. Thomas Patience Private Company B 5th Regt. Massachusetts Volunteer Cavalry (Colored). Am a pensioner under the act of Feby 6th 1907 at the rate of $15.00 per month granted Oct 31st 1910. I am now (79) seventy nine years of age or rather will be Christmas day. I have not made any claims for increase pension under the Act of May 11, 1912 because I was not informed before I saw notice in the paper. I will thank you to put me in a way to get the increase.
Respectfully,
his
Thomas X Patience"
mark

<u>Thomas Patience's Request to Commissioner of Pensions</u>

National Archives

House of Representatives U. S.

Washington, D. C.

October 19, 1914.

Hon. G. M. Saltzgaber,

    Commissioner of Pensions,

        City.

Dear Sir:-

    I beg to enclose herein application for increase of pension, under the Act of May 11, 1912, of Thomas Patience, Edenton, N.C., R. R. 1. Kindly have this application investigated with a view to early and favorable consideration. I will thank you for an acknowledgement.

                Yours very truly,

Enc.

Lawyer's Letter to Commissioner of Pensions

October 19, 1914

National Archives

3-364

ACT OF MAY 11, 1912. Cert. No. 1140754

Claimant, Thomas Patience   2484405
P.O., Edenton   Rank, Private
County, Chowan   Service, Co B
State, North Carolina   5 Mass Cav. (Colored)
Rate, $20 per month, commencing October 20, 1914
B $24 from May 13, 1915

CIVIL WAR.

ATTORNEY OR STATE REPRESENTATIVE
(Order April 25, 1907.)

Name,   Fee, $
P.O.,   Articles filed

Approved for Increase from June 10, 1918
Act of June 10, 1918 Agreed to pay Rev
JUN 12 1918

APPROVAL.

Submitted for adm. Nov 6, 1914   J S Roy, Examiner.
Approved for admission   Rate $20 per month; age 74 years.

Reissue from act February 6, 1907.

Date of birth May 13, 1840.

Length of pensionable service: 1 years, 5 months, 19 days.
Deductions in service from any cause: none years, months, days,
on account of
NOV 9 1914, 191   C M Butler Nov 9, 1914 W Waugh
                    Legal Reviewer.   Reviewer.

Enlisted May 13, 1864; honorably discharged October 31, 1865
Enlisted _____, 18 ; honorably discharged _____, 18
Enlisted _____, 18 ; honorably discharged _____, 18

Thomas Patience's Pension Increase to $24.00
Under Act of May 11, 1912
Commencing October 20, 1914
(questionable date of birth- May 13, 1840)

National Archives

3-014

ACT OF MAY 11, 1912.

DECLARATION FOR PENSION.

THE PENSION CERTIFICATE SHOULD NOT BE FORWARDED WITH THE APPLICATION.

State of **North Carolina**, County of **Chowan**, ss:

On this **17** day of **Oct** A. D. 19**14** personally appeared before me, a **Notary Public**, within and for the county and State aforesaid, **Thomas Patience** who, being duly sworn according to law, declares that he is **79** years of age, and a resident of **West Edenton** county of **Chowan**, State of **North Carolina**; and that he is the identical person who was ENROLLED at **Norfolk Va**, under the name of **Thos Patience**, on the ___ day of ___, 18__, as a **Private** in **Co B 5th Regt Massachusetts Volunteer Cav Cavalry** in the service of the United States, in the **Civil War**, and was HONORABLY DISCHARGED at **Texas** on the ___ day of ___, 18__.

That he was not employed in the military or naval service of the United States otherwise than as stated above. That his personal description at enlistment was as follows: Height, **5** feet, **8** inches; complexion, **Dark**; color of eyes, **Black**; color of hair, **Black**; that his occupation was **Laborer**; that he was born __, 18__, at **in Chowan Co N C**

That his several places of residence since leaving the service have been as follows: **always in Chowan County N C**
(State date of each change, as nearly as possible.)

That he is a pensioner under certificate No. **1,140,754**. That he has ___ applied for pension under original No. ___. That he makes this declaration for the purpose of being placed on the pension roll of the United States under the provisions of the act of May 11, 1912.

That his post-office address is **Edenton**, county of **Chowan**, State of **North Carolina**.

Attest: (1) **M. H. Dixon**

(2) _____

Thomas his **X** **Patience** ✓
mark
(Claimant's signature in full.)

SUBSCRIBED and sworn to before me this **17** day of **Oct**, A. D. 191**4**, and I hereby certify that the contents of the above declaration were fully made known and explained to the applicant before swearing, including the words ___ erased, and the words ___, added; and that I have no interest, direct or indirect, in the prosecution of this claim.

Declaration accepted as
a claim under the
act of May 11, 1912.

Chief, Law Division.

M. H. Dixon
(Signature.)
Notary Public
(Official character.)

[Stamp: U.S. PENSION OCT 20 1914]

Thomas Patience's Declaration For Pension in 1914

Under ACT OF MAY 11, 1912
October 17, 1914
National Archives
To **read content easily, turn to next page.**

ACT OF MAY 11, 1912

DECLARATION FOR PENSION

State of <u>North Carolina</u>, County of <u>Chowan</u>, 88:

"On this <u>17</u> day of <u>Oct.</u>, A.D. 19<u>14</u> personally appeared before me, a Notary Public within and for the county and State aforesaid, <u>Thomas Patience</u>, who, being duly sworn according to law, declares that he is <u>79</u> years of age and a resident of <u>near Edenton</u>, county of <u>Chowan</u>, State of <u>North Carolina</u>; and that he is the identical person who was enrolled at <u>Norfolk, VA</u>, under the name of Thos Patience, on the ___ day of ___, 18___ as a Private in <u>C B 5th Rgt Massachusetts Volunteer Col'd Cavalry</u> in the service of the United States, in the <u>Civil War</u>, and was honorably discharged at <u>Texas</u>, on the ___ day of ___, 18___.

That he was not employed in the military or naval service of the United States otherwise than as stated born_____, 18___ at in <u>Chowan Co.</u>

That his several places of residence since leaving the above. That his personal description at enlistment was as follows: Height <u>5</u> feet, <u>8</u> inches, complexion, <u>Dark</u>; color of his eyes, <u>black</u>; color of hair, <u>black</u>; that his occupation was <u>Laborer</u>; that he was service have been as follows: <u>always in Chowan County, N.C.</u>

That he is a pensioner under certificate 1.140.754...

That he makes this declaration for the purpose of being placed on the pension roll of the United States under the provisions of the act of May 11, 1912.

That his post-office address is: Edenton, county of Chowan
State of North Carolina
Attest: M. H Dixon

his
Thomas X Patience
mark

<u>Thomas Patience's Declaration For Pension in 1914</u>

ACT OF MAY 11, 1912

October 17, 1914

National Archives

THOMAS PATIENCE,
EDENTON, N.C.
1140754
ACT MAY
ROUTE 1,

3-1081
DROP REPORT—PENSIONER

.... Cert. No. ....

Pensioner ....
Soldier ....
Service ....
Class ....

RECORD DIVISION

...., 192...

In the above-described case a declaration file in this Division indicates that said pensioner died ...., 19......

Chief, Record Division.

FINANCE DIVISION
JAN 14 1930
...., 192...

The name of the above-described pensioner who was last paid at the rate of $ 65 per month to DEC 4 1929, 19......, has this day been dropped from the roll because of Death

Dec 23 1929

O. J. RANDALL
Chief, Finance Division.

Thomas Patience's Pension Drop Report

Death on December 23, 1929

(last payment- $65.00)

CHAPTER 14

VALUABLE CLUE FROM NORTH CAROLINA

Several years ago, I received a very valuable document from Earl Ijames, Curator at the North Carolina Museum of History. When I had met him some time before, I had shared my quest of locating the burial place of Pvt. Thomas Patience, 5th MA Col'd Cavalry. Earl graciously mailed me this death certificate.

Thomas Patience's Death Certificate
(courtesy of Earl Ijames, N. C. Museum of History Curator)

From studying Thomas Patience's military and pension documents, I already knew much about him, such as where he had been born and that he was a widower. New to me, however, were the cause of death and the dates of his demise and burial, albeit not revealing just where in Chowan County.

Valuable new information was his mother's name—Hester Lawrence. Furthermore, I learned that a Cornelia Lawrence had been in charge of Thomas Patience's burial. At that time, though, neither name had any meaning to me. I had not known to ask about Lawrences when I had visited Edenton—only Patiences.

Sleuths may recall seeing the name of Cornelia Lawrence already mentioned in this mystery.[92] She and husband Michael had been counted in the 1910 census as being neighbors of Thomas Patience and his wife Serena, giving rise to even more questions. In an era when women had little "say," why had Cornelia instead of her husband, Michael, been in charge of the burial of their elderly widowed neighbor?

Who might I ask such a question? I had no idea. Consequently, Thomas Patience's death certificate joined the myriad of documents I already had amassed since becoming the Patience griot. Still remaining unanswered was whether Crowder and Thomas are brothers—two Civil War veterans born in Chowan County, N.C., and having the same unusual surname "Patience."

I just might have to be satisfied with my hypothesis that they are since I knew of no way to discover the truth. That is, not until 2018 when reports from a *23andMe* DNA test[93] provided me with a list of relatives who also have taken the test. The first four I already knew: daughter Brenda, son Eric, niece Heidi, and great niece Suzanne. Cousins were listed next—the siblings Connie and Joseph Lawrence.

Suddenly it occurred to me that I had seen the name "Lawrence" somewhere before. Why, yes, I had seen it on Thomas Patience's death certificate—Hester and Cornelia Lawrence.[94]

Since *23andMe* reports that some Lawrences and Patiences share DNA, my hypothesis was confirmed. In order for siblings Connie and Joseph Lawrence to be my cousins, Thomas and Crowder Patience must be brothers.

The amount of DNA we have in common is small, making us perhaps 3rd cousins who share a set of 2nd or 3rd great grandparents. We share around 1% DNA. Located on four segments of our 10th chromosome,[95] it is enough DNA to prove that Pennsylvania Patiences and North Carolina Lawrences share ancestors from several generations back. Just how far back? For my family we can trace only to Crowder Patience who was born in Edenton, N.C.

So, just how does Thomas Patience, also born in Edenton, N.C., and whose mother is Hester Lawrence, fit into this jig-saw puzzle begun 154 years ago? Keep following carefully as the pieces begin to fit together.

Via *23andMe*, my initial correspondence with my newly-found cousins was: *"Looking for a Lawrence family relationship in Edenton, N.C."*

Joseph Lawrence Jr. responded with: *"Would like to share your knowledge of the Lawrences of Edenton."*

I requested his e-mail address so I might send him information explaining my interest in the Lawrences of Edenton, N.C. After attaching a copy of Thomas Patience's death certificate to a message, I "patiently" awaited Joseph Lawrence's response.

In the meantime, I was attempting to tie up some loose ends. Since Hester Lawrence is recorded as being Thomas Patience's mother, might she also be Crowder's? Also, who was Cornelia Lawrence to Thomas Patience for her to have been in charge of his burial? During the 1910 census count, she was listed merely as being Thomas and Serena Patience's neighbor.

Curiously, five years later in 1915, Thomas Patience would report on a pension application that he had three living children. So, where were those three children fourteen years later in 1929, so at least one of them would have arranged their own father's burial? Why had a neighbor, Cornelia Lawrence, been the one? Just how does she fit into the puzzle?

DEPARTMENT OF THE INTERIOR
BUREAU OF PENSIONS

WASHINGTON, D. C., *January 2, 1915.*

SIR: Please answer, at your earliest convenience, the questions enumerated below. The information is requested for future use, and it may be of great value to your widow or children. Use the inclosed envelope, which requires no stamp.

Very respectfully,

Gn Saley[?]
Commissioner.

THOMAS PATIENCE,
EDENTON, N.C.
1140754
ACT MAY
ROUTE 1.

U.S. PENSION OFFICE APR 14 1915

No. 1. Date and place of birth? *Answer.* ....
The name of organizations in which you served? *Answer.* ....

No. 2. What was your post office at enlistment? *Answer.* ....
No. 3. State your wife's full name and her maiden name. *Answer.* ....
No. 4. When, where, and by whom were you married? *Answer.* ....

No. 5. Is there any official or church record of your marriage? ....
If so, where? *Answer.* ....

No. 6. Were you previously married? If so, state the name of your former wife, the date of the marriage, and the date and place of her death or divorce. If there was more than one previous marriage, let your answer include all former wives. *Answer.* ....

No. 9. State the names and dates of birth of all your children, living or dead. *Answer.* ....

(Signature) *Thos. Patience*

Thomas Patience's Answer About a Wife and Children

"I have no wife and no probability of having one.
I have three children ages 47, 45, and 40 years old."

Joseph Lawrence Jr.'s return message contained this very exciting revelation: ***"Cornelia Lawrence was my great grandmother."***

GRANDFATHER- *Alexander Lawrence*

FATHER- *Joseph Lawrence Sr.*

Joseph Lawrence Jr.

<u>Four Generations of Edenton Lawrences</u>
(courtesy of Joseph's daughter Tanya Lawrence)

CHAPTER 15

THE 154-YEAR-OLD MYSTERY IS SOLVED

Unbeknownst to us both, Cousin Joe and I were about to embark on an intriguing journey to discover the ancestors we share. Hester Lawrence, for instance, was as much news to Joseph Lawrence Jr. as she had been to me. Both of us were wondering what her relationship was to his great grandmother Cornelia Lawrence and subsequently to him,

Joe's *Ancestry.com* sleuthing would lead him to the 1870 Federal Census, where he found another generation for the family tree he had created. There was 52-year-old Hester Lawrence residing in Edenton with her 77-year-old husband, Thomas Lawrence. Also, counted in that same census were 30-year-old Thos Laurence and his wife Isadora.

After reading Thomas Patience's death certificate, my inquiring mind had been dwelling on this nagging question for years: *"Might Hester Lawrence be Crowder Patience's mother, as well?"* Then because of the *23andMe* report, I began to believe she must be my link to the Lawrence family of Edenton, N.C.

Curiosity would lead Joe and me to spend hours comparing our genealogy because we wanted to know exactly how we are related. *23andMe* reports that a 2nd

or 3rd great grandparent is shared by us. If Hester Lawrence is mother to both Thomas and Crowder Patience, indeed she would be my 2nd great grandmother and Joe's 3rd. His father and I are in the same generation.

After exchanging and comparing our family histories for several weeks, Joe invited me to view his closed genealogical chart on *Ancestry.com*. Immediately, I scrolled to see who he had recorded as his first known ancestor. It was his great-great grandfather, Thomas P. Lawrence.

Next, my eyes moved to the names of Thomas P. Lawrence's two wives. Both of them had preceded him in death. They were Isadora Jones and Serena Harris.

"What!" I said to myself. **"No way!"** was my reaction to the names of Thomas Lawrence's wives.

Amazingly, "hidden in plain sight" on Cousin Joe's chart was the solution to our 154-year-old mystery! Not hidden to me, though, due to what I had read on Thomas Patience's first invalid pension application when he was being questioned about having a spouse:

*"**No. 1.** Are you a married man? If so, please state your wife's full name, and her maiden name.*
        Answer: *Yes. Serena Pations, Serina Harris*

No. 2. *When, where, and by whom were you married?*

Answer: *March 1895 at Warren's Grove Church by Rev. Sam'l Felton.*

No. 3. *What record of marriage exists?*

Answer: *License*

No. 4. *Were you previously married? If so, please state the name of your former wife and the date and place of her death or divorce.*

Answer: *Yes. Isadora died in Chowan Co. in the fall of 1894."*

Can you believe this? **THOMAS LAWRENCE AND THOMAS PATIENCE ARE ONE AND THE SAME.** Now the following questions can be answered regarding the censuses:

Q: Why, hadn't Thomas Patience been counted for the 1870 census in Edenton, N.C.?

A: He had been, but as ***Thos Laurence.*** [96]

Q: Why hadn't either Thomas Lawrence or Thomas Patience been counted on the 1880 census?

A: They had, but as a ***Thomas Larnce.*** [97]

Q. Why hadn't either Thomas Patience or Thomas Lawrence been counted for the 1900 census?

A. They had, but as ***Thomas Larnce.*** [98]

Q: Why hadn't Thomas Lawrence been counted in the 1910 census?

A: He had, but as *Thomas Patience.*[99]

Q. Why hadn't Thomas Patience been counted for the 1920 census?

A. He had, but as *Thomas Lawrence.*[100]

Sleuths who have been following closely will remember mention of the young couple, Thos Lawrence and wife Isadora, found in the 1870 census.[101] They, too, were "hidden in plain sight" along with his parents.

Because of *23andMe*, the surprising news for Patiences is that after 154 years of not knowing any other relatives, we have discovered roots intertwined with the Lawrences of Edenton, North Carolina. The surprising news for Lawrences is that one of their direct ancestors had served with the 5th MA (Col'd) Cavalry during the Civil War. His name is inscribed on the Wall of Honor in Washington, D.C. where his descendants can pay honor to him, albeit by a different surname—*Patience*.

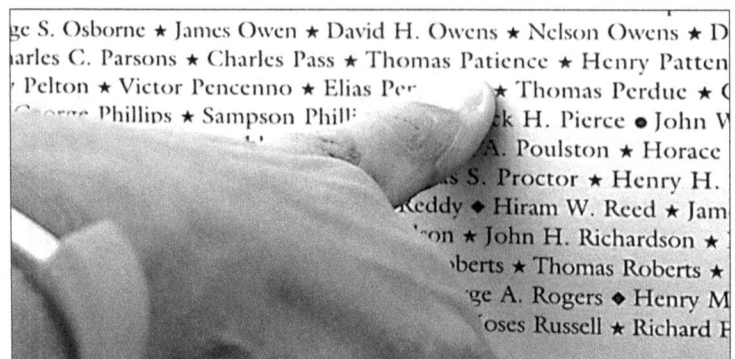

Pvt. Thomas Patience's Inscribed Name
on the Wall of Honor
(photo by Reba N. Burruss-Barnes, Publicist)
May 30, 2018

CHAPTER 16
CONCLUDING EVIDENCE

Like many other stalwart young Blacks, Thomas Lawrence/Patience had absconded from bondage to fight for the freedom of his family and neighbors. Certainly he is deserving of a memorial where it can be seen and honored by family and others alike. But where was he laid to rest?

Joseph Lawrence Jr. may have that answer. He says that when he was very young, his great grandmother Cornelia had lived with his family in Edenton until she passed away in 1960. Cousin Joe remembers her being laid to rest on the property willed to her by husband, Michael. His death certificate states that his burial was in Chowan County in 1927, as so states Thomas Patience's in 1929. Neither death certificate mentions a cemetery, though. Might both her husband and her father-in-law be buried on Cornelia Lawrence's property as well?

Still one wonders why Cornelia was the one to have arranged her father-in-law's burial. Since the 1920 census had counted the widower Thomas Lawrence as residing with the family of his son, James, why had he not been the one to arrange his father's burial nine years later?

The reason was that James had passed away in July 1929, just five months prior to his father's death in December. Subsequently, after the deaths of her husband Michael and his brother James, Cornelia Wilder Lawrence became the matriarch of the Lawrence family.

****

Thomas and Crowder fled from bondage in 1863 soon after the Yankees began penetrating the South. The two would add to the burgeoning number of fugitives who were equated with lost revenue. So the return of its "property" was of utmost importance to the Confederacy. To avoid the dire consequences of such a fate, many contrabands[102] chose new names to avoid being associated with their former owners. For such a reason might Thomas and Crowder have chosen "Patience" as theirs?

When Thomas returned home in 1867, he immediately was recognized by neighbors who knew him before he had absconded. Years later, however, he would need affidavits from them to attest to the fact that the returning soldier was indeed the same man who had left four years prior. By which surname he was addressed in Edenton—Lawrence or Patience—may have been of little importance to the veteran until his need of a government disability pension. Then he would be obliged to use the name recorded on his military records.

Friends were asked to submit affidavits for him because as Thomas Lawrence, he could never receive an invalid pension, but as Thomas Patience/Pashons, he just might—and did.

Among the many documents in the possession of Joseph Lawrence Jr. are receipts bearing his 2nd great-grandfather Thomas Lawrence's name. The following is a "part payment" of $11.00 on a note dated Dec. 2, 1889.

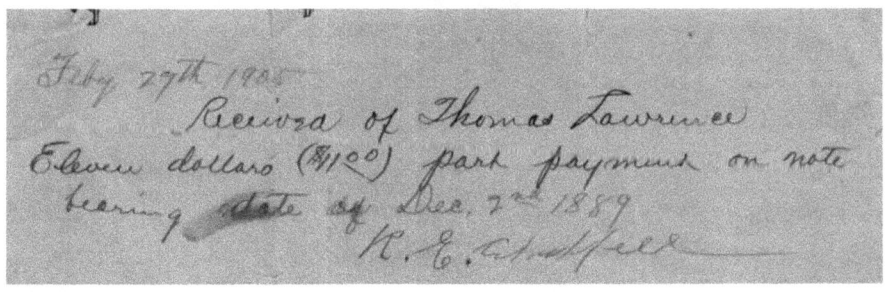

<u>Thomas Lawrence's Receipt</u>
Dated February 27, 1905
(courtesy of Joseph Lawrence Jr.)

In addition to the receipts is a document promising repayment after a successful harvest. Such a document is called a "Chattel Mortgage." [103] Found on this document is the name "Thomas Patience." With astonishment, Joe admits that as many times as he had seen these papers, the name "Patience" never caught his eye.

<u>Thomas Patience's Chattel Mortgage Receipt</u>
Thos X Patience
Dated November 1, 1910
(courtesy of Joseph Lawrence Jr.)

A Chattel Mortgage for Thomas Patience in 1910

(courtesy of Joseph Lawrence Jr.)

The Chattel Mortgage Marked Paid

Signed by H. C. Privott

(courtesy of Joseph Lawrence Jr.)

To read content easily, turn to next page.

CHATTEL MORTGAGE

"I, <u>Thos Patience</u> of the County of <u>Chowan</u>, State of North Carolina am indebted to H.C. PRIVOTT, of Chowan County, said state, in the sum of <u>Twenty-five</u> _____ Dollars for which <u>he</u> holds <u>my</u> note, to be due on the <u>1</u> day of <u>Nov.</u> A.D. 19<u>10</u> and to secure the payment <u>I</u> hereby convey to <u>him</u> these articles of personal property, to wit.

One bay mare mule. One best cart wheels and gear complete. All my farming implements and any other chattel property I own or may own including all crops that may raised by or for me this year on my own land or elsewhere in said county.

But on this special Trust that if <u>I</u> fail to pay said debt and interest on or before the <u>1</u> day of <u>Nov.</u> A.D. 19<u>10</u>, then <u>he</u> may sell said property, or so much thereof may be necessary by PUBLIC AUCTION FOR CASH, first giving twenty days' notice at three public places, and apply the proceeds of such sale to the discharge of said debt and interest on the same, and cost of collection and pay any surplus to <u>me</u>.

Given by <u>my</u> hand and seal on this <u>10</u> day of <u>Mch</u> A.D. 19<u>10</u>

Witness:

W.B. Stillman

his
Thos X Patience
mark

<u>Chattel Mortgage Marked Paid</u>

Signed by H. C. Privott

(courtesy of Joseph Lawrence Jr.)

CHAPTER 17

QUESTIONS STILL UNANSWERED

23andMe reveals that Joseph Lawrence Jr. and I have some DNA in common. According to the reports, we share 2nd or 3rd great grandparents. The only conceivable way is if the two Patience Civil War soldiers, Thomas and Crowder, are brothers.

Both the Lawrences and the Patiences are families deeply rooted in Edenton, North Carolina. Exactly just how many generations deep, is not known at this time.

After the Civil War had ended, Pvt. Thomas Patience would return to those roots. Pvt. Crowder Patience would not, but 154 years later, thanks to new genealogical resources such as *23andMe* and *Ancestry.com*, some of his descendants now are researching their North Carolina roots.

Still, unanswered questions remain, such as:

1. Why had both Thomas and Crowder used the surname "Patience" when enlisting in the Union Army?

2. Was Thomas's father's surname "Patience," as is recorded on the veteran's pension applications? [104]

3. Was Crowder originally "Tobe," as my Uncle Bob had said?

5. If so, then why was "Crowder" his chosen name as a free man?

Perhaps someone else will find the answers and close this 154-year-old mystery with a proper *FINIS*.

LAWRENCE/PATIENCE GENERATIONS

The 1st survived,

The 2nd did not talk,

The 3rd did not ask,

The 4th wondered,

The 5th researched,

The 6th preserved,

The 7th respected,

The 8th shares,

The 9th continues.

WHY?

So future generations can know their history.

(inspired by Cheryl Chevalier Ph.D.)

CHAPTER 18
IN MEMORIAM

Joseph Lawrence Jr. Locates His Ancestor's Name On the Wall
May 30, 2018
(photo by Reba N. Burruss-Barnes, Publicist)

Lawrence Family
Seated: *Mother- Regina, Granddaughter-Deja, Daughter-Tanya*
Standing: *Father-Joseph, Daughter-Cynthia*

(courtesy of Joseph Lawrence Jr.)

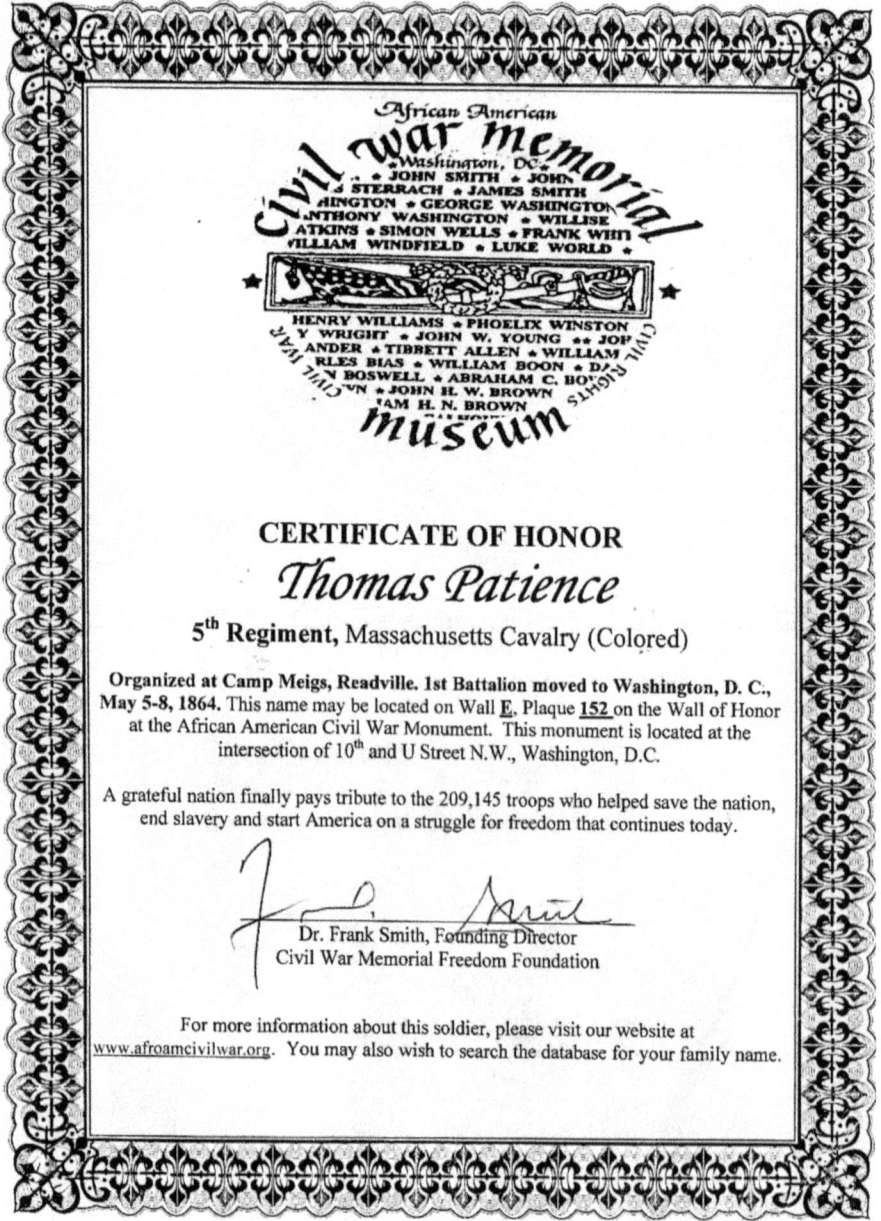

Certificate of Honor for Pvt. Thomas Patience

**African American Civil War Museum
Washington, D.C.
*(opened July 1998)***

Two Civil War Brothers

by Joel Ulmer

J.innovinci@gmail.com

2018

Privates Thomas and Crowder Patience

On this final day of 2018 when jokingly some people might be planning their New Year's resolutions, Cousin Joseph R. Lawrence Jr. and I are seriously committing to one. For it is our desire that during the year 2019, a memorial will be placed in the Providence African American Cemetery in Edenton, N.C., for remembering the two young slave brothers who had escaped their bondage to serve in the Union Army during the Civil War to gain freedom.

The younger, Crowder Patience, served with the 103rd Pennsylvania Volunteers while the elder, Thomas Patience/Lawrence served in the 5th MA (Col'd) Cavalry. The two brothers were separated, never to meet again. Serendipitously, many years later, they would die within a month of each other. Crowder is buried in the West Pittston Cemetery in West Pittston, Pennsylvania. Thomas is buried in Chowan County, N.C., exact site speculative.

Many gravesites of those who have served in the military are identified and honored by tombstones provided by the U.S. Government. Crowder's is so marked in Pennsylvania; Thomas' has not been in North Carolina. Therefore, it is our desire that the two Edenton brothers might be remembered together by a memorial in a spot easily seen by their descendants and other interested persons.

APPENDIX I

Tracing the Lawrence/Patience Y-Chromosome

Paternal Ancestry

(Courtesy of LeRoy Crowder Patience Jr.)

PATIENCES	LAWRENCES
1st generation	
A kidnapped unknown male from Cameroon	
2nd known generation in Edenton, N.C.	
Thomas David Lawrence Sr.	
3rd generation	
Crowder Patience	Thomas D. Lawrence Jr. Patience
4th generation	
Percy Patience	Michael L. Lawrence
5th generation	
LeRoy Crowder Patience Sr.	Alexander H. Lawrence
6th generation	
LeRoy Crowder Patience Jr.	Joseph R. Lawrence Sr.
7th generation	
Keenan Patience	Joseph R. Lawrence Jr.
8th generation	
Zachary Patience	
9th generation	
Jayden Patience	

APPENDIX II

FIRST GENERATIONS OF PENNSYLVANIA PATIENCES

1st Gen.	2nd Gen.	3rd Gen.
CROWDER m. ELSIE VEDEN	FLORENCE m. Walter Kirk Glover.	Rosa Mae (Jackson) Elsie Veden (Andrews) Walter Kirk Harry Brazier Jessie Pearl Edward Charles Niles Robert Florence Patience (Smith)
	HARRY B. m. Elsie Miller	Robert Jesse Kenneth Veden Wilmer Miller Charles Edgar Harry Bruce Harold Lee
	ROSA VEDEN m. Simon Peter Lee	none
	LILLIAN MARIA m. Charles E. Cuff	none
	JESSIE PEARL m. Nathaniel Garrett	none
	PERCY m. Mary Adams	Ruth (Norman) Dorothy (Watson) LeRoy Crowder Thomas Lillian Mae Charles Stanley
	CHESTER D. m. Edna Lucas	Chester Douglas Bernice Lee
	NILES m. Edna Gaylord	none

APPENDIX III

Presentation Pedigree of Matthew Allen Patience

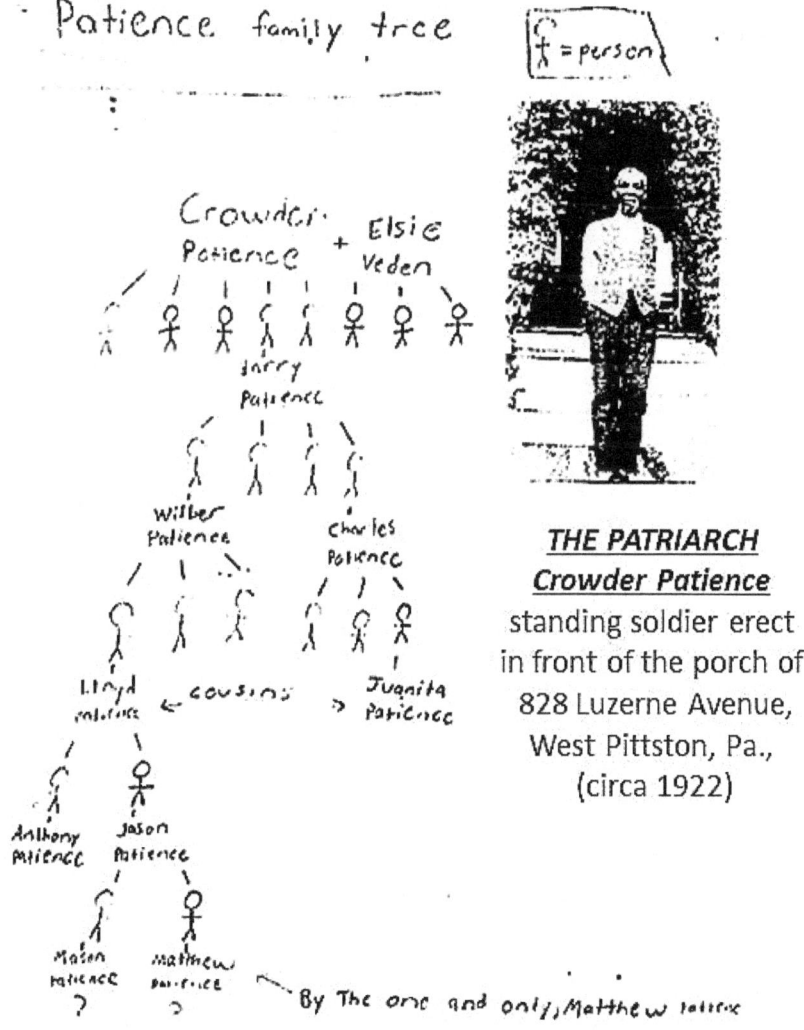

THE PATRIARCH
Crowder Patience
standing soldier erect
in front of the porch of
828 Luzerne Avenue,
West Pittston, Pa.,
(circa 1922)

PATERNAL GENEALOGY OF
MATTHEW ALLEN PATIENCE

GENERATIONS:

8th   Matthew Allen Patience- son of:

7th   Jason Patience- son of:

6th   Lloyd Albert Patience- son of:

5th   Wilmer Miller Patience- son of:

4th   Harry Brazier Patience- son of:

3rd   Crowder Patience- son of:

2nd   Thomas David Lawrence Sr.- son of:

1st   **Male Ancestor kidnapped from Cameroon**

APPENDIX IV

Pedigree of Joseph R. Lawrence Jr.

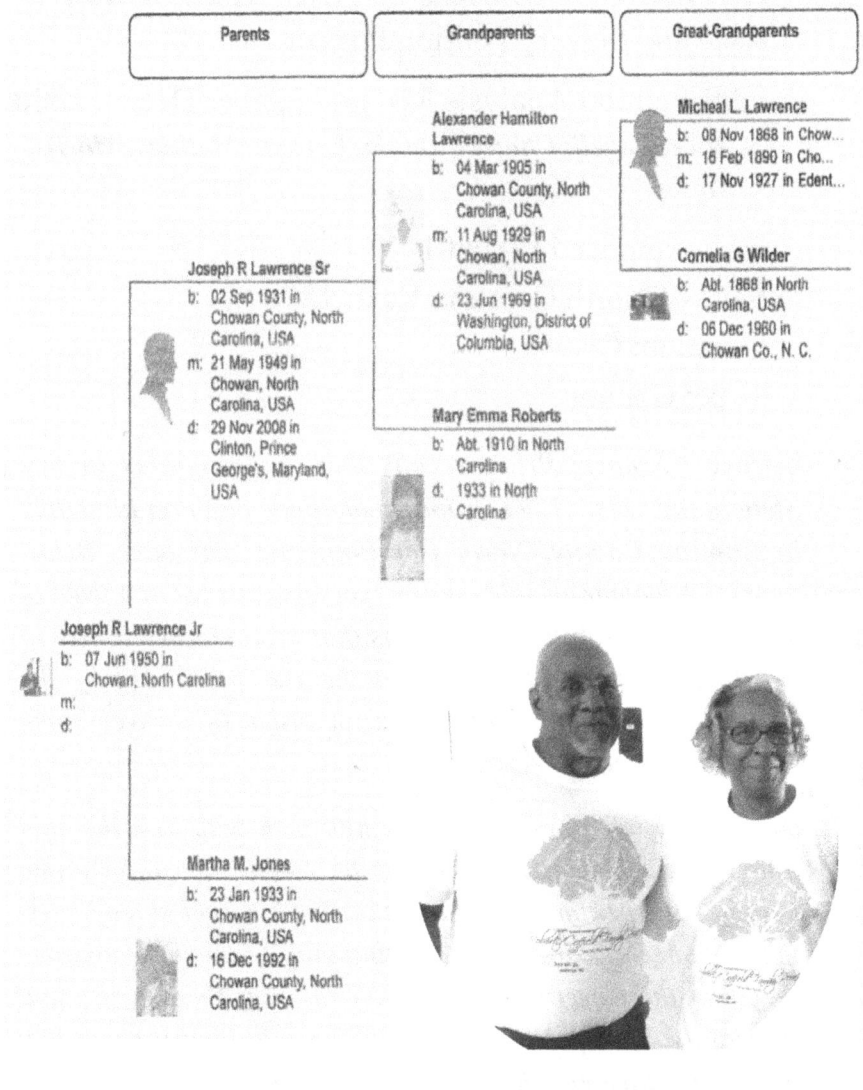

Parents	Grandparents	Great-Grandparents
Joseph R Lawrence Sr b: 02 Sep 1931 in Chowan County, North Carolina, USA m: 21 May 1949 in Chowan, North Carolina, USA d: 29 Nov 2008 in Clinton, Prince George's, Maryland, USA	**Alexander Hamilton Lawrence** b: 04 Mar 1905 in Chowan County, North Carolina, USA m: 11 Aug 1929 in Chowan, North Carolina, USA d: 23 Jun 1969 in Washington, District of Columbia, USA	**Micheal L. Lawrence** b: 08 Nov 1868 in Chow... m: 16 Feb 1890 in Cho... d: 17 Nov 1927 in Edent...
	Mary Emma Roberts b: Abt. 1910 in North Carolina d: 1933 in North Carolina	**Cornelia G Wilder** b: Abt. 1868 in North Carolina, USA d: 06 Dec 1960 in Chowan Co., N. C.

Joseph R Lawrence Jr
b: 07 Jun 1950 in Chowan, North Carolina
m:
d:

Martha M. Jones
b: 23 Jan 1933 in Chowan County, North Carolina, USA
d: 16 Dec 1992 in Chowan County, North Carolina, USA

<u>Lawrence Siblings</u>

Joseph and Connie

2018

(courtesy of Joseph R. Lawrence, Jr.)

APPENDIX V

RE: FRANCOIS BRIOLS AND NINE SLAVES
Race and Slavery Petition Project

PAR Petition Analysis Record Number Dec. 4, 1806

> Alice, Bagell, Charles, Desda, Lewbin. Mathias, Morris, Moses

PAR Number 11280601
State of North Carolina Year: 1806
Location: Chowan
Type: County

Abstract: *"Francis Briols recalls that 'he emigrated in this State in the year...1794' from Guadaloupe and that he settled in Chowan County, North Carolina: one year later, Briols married a woman in said county 'possessed in fee of a tract of land and nine slaves.' He submits that he continued to live in North Carolina until 1802 when he was persuaded by his friends to return to Guadaloupe in order to recover some valuable property.*

Briols left Chowan County and took with him the said nine slaves. Having found that he 'made an unfortunate change,' the petitioner declares that 'he has ever since he left the State been desirous of returning and is now more anxious to do so than ever.' Briols, understanding that the present laws of the State prohibit the importation of Slaves, prays that a law be passed enabling him 'to return in this State with the same Nine Negroes & children he carried away, and no other.'"

APPENDIX VI

Petition Granted to Francois Briols

From: General Assembly Session Records, Nov-Dec. 1806
Joint Committee Propositions & Grievances

To read more easily, go to next page.

Petition is Granted to Francois Briols

"The Committee of Props & Grievances to whom was referred the Petiion of Francois Briols of the Island of Guadaloupe praying authority to bring into this State certain Negroes

Report

That your Committee are of opinion from representations to them made that the petitioner's prayer is reasonable and ought to be granted. Therefore recommend the Bill accompanying this Report entitled "A Bill to Authorize Francois Briols of the Island of Guadaloupe to bring into this State certain Negroes therein mentioned to be passed into a Law."

APPENDIX VII

FORMATION OF UNITED STATES COLORED TROOPS

GENERAL ORDERS, } WAR DEPARTMENT,
ADJUTANT GENERAL'S OFFICE,
No. 143. } *Washington, May 22, 1863.*

I. A Bureau is established in the Adjutant General's Office for the record of all matters relating to the organization of Colored Troops. An officer will be assigned to the charge of the Bureau, with such number of clerks as may be designated by the Adjutant General.

II, III, IV, V.

VI. Colored troops may be accepted by companies, to be afterwards consolidated in battalions and regiments by the Adjutant General. The regiments will be numbered seriatim, in the order in which they are raised, the numbers to be determined by the Adjutant General They will be designated: "—Regiment of U.S. Colored Troops."

VII. Recruiting stations and depots will be established by the Adjutant General as circumstances shall require, and officers will be detailed to muster and inspect the troops.

APPENDIX VIII

GENERAL ORDERS No. 323

WAR DEPT., ADJT. GENERAL'S OFFICE,

Washington, September 28, 1863

"In section 10, act of March 3, 1863, it is enacted:

that the President of the United States be, and he is hereby authorized to cause to be enlisted for each cook (to allowed by section 9) two undercooks of African descent, who shall receive for their full compensation $10 per month and one ration per day; $3 of said monthly pay may be in clothing.

For a regular company, the two undercooks will be enlisted; for a volunteer company, they will be mustered into service, as in the cases of other soldiers. In each case a remark will be made on their enlistment papers showing that they are undercooks of African descent. Their names will be borne on the company muster-rolls at the foot of the list of privates. They will be paid, and their accounts will be kept, like other enlisted men. They will also be discharged in the same manner as other soldier."

By order of the Secretary of War:
E. D. TOWNSEND,
Assistant Adjutant-General

NOTES

1. Griot [pronounced gree-o], a storyteller in West African cultures.

PREFACE

2. Named for the 23 pairs of chromosomes found in human cells. It is a privately held personal genomics and biotechnology company based in Mountain View, California. https://en.wikipedia.org/wiki/

3. The steel-plated Wall of Honor surrounding the 11-foot bronze "Spirit of Freedom" in Washington, D.C. It is located at the Mount Vernon Plaza at the Shaw Metro Station.

4. The "Spirit of Freedom," centerpiece of the African American Civil War Memorial, is the only national memorial to honor the contributions of Civil War Black soldiers and sailors. The African American Civil War Memorial Freedom Foundation and Museum is located at 1925 Vermont Ave. NW, Washington, D.C.

INTRODUCTION

5. Moss. *Deeply Rooted*, 119. According Thomas Patience's death certificate, he was buried in Chowan County, but no actual burial site is given.

6. Appendix 1: The Y- chromosome is found only in males and is passed unchanged to male descendants. Therefore, the paternal ancestry of a family may be traced back for generations by the genetic makeup of the Y- chromosome.

Through *Ancestry.com* LeRoy Crowder Patience Jr. traced his Patience Y- chromosome to the Language People [haplogroup E3a] who may have lived in Cameroon or Benin.

Chapter 1
The Pennsylvania Patiences

7. Located on the Albemarle Sound, Edenton is one of the first permanent European settlements in North Carolina. Settled in 1658, it was incorporated in 1727. Because of the many "Unionists" in residence, the lovely town was spared destruction during the Civil War, unlike Plymouth, N.C., where the majority of buildings were destroyed during the alternating occupations of Confederate and Union forces there.

8. "Colored" and "Black" are used interchangeably throughout this book, depending upon era and circumstances.

9. Belinda Hurmence, *My Folks Don't Want Me to Talk About Slavery: Twenty-one Histories of Former North Carolina Slaves,* (John F. Blair, Publisher: Winston-Salem, N.C., 1984).

10. "Civil War Veteran of Unusual Career is Valley Resident," Wilkes-Barre *Sunday Independent*, May 20, 1928. Juanita Patience Moss, *Created to Be Free*, (Willow Bend Books: Westminster, Md., 2001), x.

11. Guests at Lillian Patience Cuff's 98th birthday party in Montclair, New Jersey, in 1981.

Front row (L-R):
1. **Jennifer Patience-** Chester Douglas Patience Sr.'s granddaughter; Chester Douglas Patience Jr.'s daughter
2. **Davis Henry Jr.-** Harold Lee Patience Sr.'s grandson; Marian Patience Henry's son
3. **Lillian Maria Patience Cuff-** Crowder Patience's daughter
4. **Robert Jesse Patience-** Crowder Patience's grandson; Harry Brazier Patience's son
5. **Elsie Betty Patience Claiborne-** Harry Brazier Patience's granddaughter; Wilmer Miller Patience's daughter
6. **Anthony Patience-** Wilmer Miller Patience's grandson; Lloyd Albert Patience's son
7. **Jason Patience-** Wilmer Patience's grandson; Lloyd Albert Patience's son

Back rows (L-R):
8. **Sandra Patience**- Chester Douglas Patience Sr.'s granddaughter; Chester Douglas Patience Jr.'s daughter
9. **Beryl Patience** - Chester Douglas Patience Jr.'s wife
10. **Chester Douglas Patience Jr.**– Crowder Patience's grandson; Chester Douglas Patience Sr.'s son
11. **Ethel Sample Patience** – Robert Jesse Patience's wife
12. **Juanita Bernice Patience Moss** – Harry Brazier Patience's granddaughter; Charles Edgar Patience's daughter
13. **Carol Norman Jackson**- Percy Patience's granddaughter; Ruth Patience Norman's daughter
14. **Marian Henry**- Harold Lee Patience Sr.'s granddaughter; Marian Patience Henry's daughter
15. **Cynthia Kennedy Wade**- Kenneth Veden Patience's granddaughter; Katherine Patience Kennedy's daughter
16. **Harold Lee Patience Jr.**– Harry Brazier Patience's grandson; Harold Lee Patience Sr.'s son
17. **Marian Patience Henry**- Harry Brazier Patience's granddaughter; Harold Lee Patience Sr.'s daughter
18. **Bernice Lee Patience** – Crowder Patience's granddaughter; Chester Douglas Patience Sr.'s daughter
19. **Douglas Patience**- Chester Douglas Patience Sr.'s grandson; Chester Douglas Jr.'s son
20. **Florence Patience Glover Smith** – Crowder Patience's granddaughter; Florence Patience Glover's daughter
21. **LeRoy Crowder Patience Jr.**- Percy Patience's grandson; LeRoy Crowder Patience Sr.'s son
22. **Katherine Patience Kennedy**- Harry Brazier Patience's granddaughter; Kenneth Veden Patience's daughter
23. **Lucius Kennedy**- Katherine Patience Kennedy's husband
24. **Lloyd Albert Patience**- Harry Brazier Patience's grandson; Wilmer Miller Patience's son
25. **Rosalind Mason Patience**- Lloyd Albert Patience's wife

Chapter 2
What's In A Name?

12. "Decoration Day" had its origin with placing of flowers on the graves of the Civil War dead. Several groups have claimed to be the first. The first National holiday took place at Arlington Cemetery on May 30, 1868, and it honored both Union and Confederate soldiers.

In 1968 when the U.S. Government passed the Uniform Monday Holiday Act, the name was officially changed to Memorial Day. It became a holiday for remembering those who served in all wars. The date was established for the last Monday of May in order to provide a long weekend for Government workers.

13. The G.A.R. (Grand Army of the Republic) was a fraternal organization of Civil War Veterans. Its symbol was a star whose five points represented the five branches of the Union military: Artillery, Cavalry, Infantry, Marines, and Navy.

14. Moss, *Deeply Rooted,* 52.

Chapter 3
Pvt. Crowder Pacien The Soldier

15. Union troops under General Ambrose E. Burnside captured Roanoke Island on February 8, 1862. Until the end of the war, it would remain a stronghold of Union troops that included detached companies from the regiments garrisoned at Plymouth. The Freedmen's Colony would function there from 1862-67. It received over 3,000 contrabands whose numbers would increase following the Union defeat at Plymouth, April 17-20, 1864.
Patricia C. Click, *Time Full of Trial: The Roanoke Island Freedmen's Colony, 1862-1867*, (University of North Carolina Press: Chapel Hill, N.C., 2001), 128.
Weymouth T. Jordan and Gerald W. Thomas, "Massacre at Plymouth," *The North Carolina Historical Review*, Vol. LXXII, April 1956, 127.

Juanita Patience Moss, *Battle of Plymouth, N.C., April 17-20, 1864: The Last Confederate Victory,* (Heritage Books: Berwyn Heights. Md., 2003), 115.

16. An ironclad ship built in a cornfield near Scot's Landing, N.C., located on the Roanoke River. Built narrow enough to be able to steam down the Roanoke River, the *CSS Albemarle* was able to surprise and then defeat the Yankees garrisoned at Plymouth. Six months later it was torpedoed by Lieut. William Barker Cushing and put out of commission. Plymouth was retaken by the Yankees who remained there for duration of the war.
Robert G. Elliot, *Ironclad of the Roanoke; Gilbert Elliot's Albemarle,* (Shippensburg, Pa.: White Mane Publishing Co., Inc., 1999).

17. Built in haste after General Ulysses S. Grant suddenly ceased prisoner-of-war exchanges. The Confederates were insisting that captured Black soldiers be remanded back to slavery and not treated as prisoners-of-war. General Grant refused.

18. Historic marker in front of the Port 'O Plymouth Museum at the intersection of East Water Street and Madison Street, Plymouth, N.C.

19. Jordan and Thomas, 192.

20. *Roster of the 103rd Pennsylvania Regiment.*
http://users.aol.com/EvanSlaughrostp.html

21. Nickname given by the Confederates to the defeated Yankees from Plymouth, N.C. When marching into the infamous Andersonville Prison, they were attired in their dress uniforms. Seems that the "Hardee" hats worn by some of the Yankees reminded their captors of the Pilgrims of Plymouth, Massachusetts. Wayne Mahood, *Charlie Mosher's Civil War: From Fair Oaks to Andersonville with the Plymouth Pilgrims (85th N.Y. Infantry),* (Longstreet House: Hightstown, N.J., 1994), 205.

22. Confederate President Jefferson Davis' statement eight days before the Emancipation Proclamation became effective that: *"All negro slaves captured in arms be at once delivered over to the executive authorities of the respective States to which they belong."*

John Dwight Warner, Jr., *Crossed Sabres: A History of the Fifth Massachusetts Volunteer Cavalry, An African American Regiment in the Civil War,* A Dissertation, Boston College, The Graduate School of Arts and Sciences, May 1997, 57.

23. No mercy was to be shown to the defeated. At Fort Pillow, Tenn., on April 12, 1864, while attempting to surrender, Black soldiers were shown no mercy by Confederate soldiers under the command of Major-General Nathan Bedford Forrest. Afterwards *"Remember Fort Pillow"* became a rallying call for Black soldiers.

24. Soldiers fighting in an actual battle.

25. Luther Dickey, *History of the 103rd Regiment: Pennsylvania Volunteer Infantry 1861-1865,* (Chicago, Illinois: L. S. Dickey, 1910), 84.

26. Ron Gancus, *The Hardship Regiment: The Penna.103rd,* (Butler, Pa.: Meching Bookbinding, 1998), 13.

27. Anthracite coal Keystone Plaque carved by Charles Edgar Patience who created many trophies for dignitaries and visitors to the anthracite area. He was always addressed by his middle name "Edgar."
Juanita Patience Moss. *Anthracite Coal Art by Charles Edgar Patience.* (Westminster, Md.: Heritage Books, 2006), 93.

Chapter 4
Crowder Patience The Citizen

28. Marriage license for Crowder Patient and Elsie Veden on August 4, 1874, in Mechanicsburg, Pennsylvania, at the Evangelical Lutheran Church.

29. Anthracite coal heart-shaped pendant attributed to C. Edgar Patience." Curator Joanne Hyppolite Ph.D. *A Century in the Making* exhibition at the National Museum of African American History and Culture, Washington, D.C.
   httpps://mnaahc.si.ed/object/nmaahc_2016.70.2

30. Card for Harry B. Patience's business of manufacturing different kinds of coal novelties. Self-taught, he trained his three younger brothers first and in later years, his six sons. Two only, Charles Edgar and Harold Lee. would continue carving anthracite

throughout their entire lives. Harold Lee Patience Sr. served in the United States Army during World War II and was wounded during the battle at Anzio Beachhead, Italy.

31. Elsie Veden was one of many bound [indentured] children orphaned by smallpox epidemics in Washington, D.C., and Virginia during the 1860s. Many, like the author's great grandmother Elsie, were placed by religious organizations into the homes of families who promised to impart good habits, morality, strong work ethics, etc. while the orphans "worked for their keep." Oftentimes the duration would end at sixteen years of age, as did Elsie's in Dillsburg, Pennsylvania.

Paula Tarnapol Whitacre, *A Civil Life in an Uncivil Time, Julia Wilbur's Struggle for Purpose,* (Potomac Books: University of Nebraska Press, 2017), 114-115.

First Annual Report, National Association, Relief of Destitute, Colored Woman and Children, (McGill & Witherow, Printers and Stereotypers: Washington, D.C., 1864), 2- 3.

32. Hurmence, ix. In the 1930s the Federal Writer's Project was created by the government to employ jobless writers to interview over 2,000 ex-slaves so their stories would be told before all were lost. *Slave Narratives* is the result and is stored at the Library of Congress.

33. Hardest of all coals and found in the United States only in northeastern Pennsylvania.

EBONY, March 1970, Carolyn DuBose, "Coal Black Art," 92-96.
Moss. *Anthracite Coal Art by Charles Edgar Patience,* 7.

34. Appendix II; Genealogy of Three Patience Generations.

35. A boundary determined in 1767 by the English surveyors Charles Mason and Jeremiah Dixon who were hired by the Penn and Calvert families to settle their dispute over the boundaries between Pennsylvania and Maryland. The boundary was settled at a northern latitude of 39 degrees and 43 minutes. Years later, it was used to distinguish between slave owning and non-slave owning states, Maryland and Delaware being the former and Pennsylvania the latter.

36. *Sunday Independent,* Wilkes-Barre, Pa., May 28, 1928.

37. Appendix VI: The petition was granted to Francois Briols.

38. John Hope Franklin and Loren Schweninger, *Runaway Slaves: Rebels on the Plantation, (*Oxford University Press: New York, 1999), 210, 213.

39. Moss*, Deeply Rooted*, 37.

40. Moss, *Created to Be Free*, vii-x.

41. Harriet Jacobs, *Incidents in the Life of a Slave Girl,* edited by Ellen Fagan Yellin, (Cambridge, Massachusetts: Harvard University Press, 1987).

After escaping to New York and becoming an abolitionist, Harriet Jacobs wrote her autobiography that was published in 1861. During the Civil War, she and her daughter were prominent in aiding contrabands in Alexandria, Va.

42. Uncontrollable coughing.

43. Influenza.

44. *Pittston Gazette.* January 31, 1930, 7.

45. *Ibid.* February 4, 1930, 7.

46. A walkway created with donors' bricks, each inscribed with the name of a Civil War soldier.

Chapter 5
Black Soldiers In The Civil War

47. Appendix IV. General Orders 323.

48. Drove wagons to carry supplies as well as the artillery into battle.

49. Took care of horses' hooves and their shoeing, as well as the general health of the animals. During the Civil War horses suffered from various illnesses and neither side had veterinarians. "Veterinary Medical Care During the Civil War." https://civilwartalk.com/threads/veterinary-medical-care-during-the civil -war.130226/

50. Traveling with forges, fashioned the horse shoes for the farriers' use and repaired wagons as well as metal equipment. "Blacksmithing During the Civil War." https://www.americancivilwarforum.com/blacksmith-during-the-acw-1944615.html

51. Made and repaired saddles.

52. The name of Medal of Honor recipient Pvt. Bruce Anderson is not inscribed on the Wall of Honor in Washington, D.C., since he had not served in one of the segregated regiments. Rather, he served in the 142nd NY Infantry Co. K. He is buried in the Greenhill Cemetery, Amsterdam, N.Y.

Juanita Moss, *Forgotten Black Soldiers Who Served in White Regiments During the Civil War.* Revised, (Heritage Books, Inc.: Berwyn Heights, Md., 2008), 162.

_____, *Forgotten Black Soldiers Who Served in White Regiments During the Civil War.* Vol. II, (Heritage Books, Inc.: Berwyn Heights, Md., 2014), 22, 23, 35, 158.

53. "Black Soldiers in the U.S. Military During The Civil War." https:www.archives.gov/education/lessons/blacks-civil-war

54. "Unionists," such as the members the 1st AL Cavalry were Southerners loyal to the United States of America. Every Confederate state except South Carolina raised at least one Union regiment.

55. From the National Archives in Washington, D.C, *Ancestry.com* has retrieved the names of Civil War soldiers by their ranks, regiments, and companies.

56. Moss. *FBS.* Vol. II, 94.

Chapter 6
Pvt. Thomas Patience On The Wall Of Honor

57. Black sculptor from Lexington, Kentucky, and also known for his Amistad Memorial in New Haven, Connecticut.

Chapter 7
Pvt. Thomas Patience The Soldier

58. Broadfoot Publishing Company located in Wilmington, N.C. specializes in multivolume reference sets for libraries and genealogical facilities.

59. Persons who were illiterate had no signature, so often used the letter "X" as their "mark" to indicate they understood what was being asked of them and were in agreement. Witnesses often were present.

60. Steven M. LaBarre, *The Fifth Massachusetts Colored Cavalry in the Civil War,* (McFarland Co., Inc.: Jefferson, N.C., 1976), 64.

61. John Dwight Warner, Jr., *Crossed Sabres: A History of the Fifth Massachusetts Volunteer Cavalry, An African American Regiment in the Civil War.*

62. LaBarre, 40-41, 116.

63. *Ibid*, 39.

64. Warner, 240.

65. LaBarre, 115.

66. The first Confiscation Act was passed on August 6, 1861. It authorized Union seizure of rebel property. That would include slaves who had fought with or worked for the Confederate military services. All were freed from any obligations to former owners.

67. LaBarre, 117.

68. James McPherson. The Negro's Civil War. (New York: Ballentine Books, 1990), 241.

69. Benjamin Quarles. *The Negro in the Civil War. (*A Da Capo Paperback, New York: A Subsidiary of Plenum Publishing Corp., 1953), 331.

70. LaBarre. 125. *Richmond Whig*. April 4, 1865.

71. Used for a supply post by the United States during the Mexican War. Brazos de Santiago was located at the southern tip of Texas ten miles from the border of Mexico.

72. Nick Salvatore, *We All Got History: The Memory Books of Amos Webber,* (Times Books: New York, 1996), 146.

73. An inducement fee offered for enlistments. Quotas were set up by the states and if the needed numbers had not been met, oftentimes bounties were offered to nonresidents as occurred with the 5th MA (Col'd) Cavalry.

74. Appendix III

Chapter 8
Confusing Surname Spellings
[none]

Chapter 9
The Brother Who Returned Home

75. Based on extent of disabilities incurred during military service. "1890 Civil War Veterans Pensions." *The Atlantic Monthly* https://www.seniorliving.org/history/1890-civil-war-veterans-pension/

Chapter 10
Thomas Patience The Citizen

76. Found in Article 1, Section 2, Clause 3 of the United States Constitution:

"Representatives and direct Taxes shall be apportioned among the several States which may be included within this Union, according to their respective Numbers, which shall be determined by adding to the whole Number of free Persons, including those bound to Service for a Term of Years, and excluding Indians not taxed, three fifths of all other Persons."

77. The license for the marriage of Thomas Lawrence and Serena Harris records that it took place on March 18, 1898, at the Warren Grove Baptist Church in Edenton, N.C.

Chapter 11
Pension Applications and Affidavits

78. United States Civil War Pension Records (National Institute) https://www.familysearch.org/wiki/en/United_States_Civil_War_Pension_Record_(National_Institute)

79. *Ibid.*

80. A crackling or rattling sound in joints.

81. Rating system used by medical examiners to form judgments concerning the granting of pensions based on the degree of a particular disability.

82. *Ibid.* Indicated declining health.

83. United States Civil War Pension Records. Moss, *Deeply Rooted*. 35.

Chapter 12
Revelations Found on Pension Applications

84. Moss, *Deeply Rooted*, 37.
85. *Ibid*, 111, 112.
86. *Ibid*, 119.
87. Located at 119 East Gale Street in Edenton, N.C., and built in 1897 by the Black carpenter Hannibal Badham and his two sons. Already much in need of repair, the edifice was rendered unsafe for worship after Hurricane Isabel damaged it in 2003. The congregation has since moved to a new location.
88. *Historic Edenton and Chowan County Guide Book*, 71.
89. The Chowan County Courthouse, Edenton, N.C., is located at 117 East King Street and is a National Historic Landmark.
Photo from www.vistedenton.com/sites,php

Chapter 13
Thomas Patience's Pension Increases

90. Moss, *Deeply Rooted*. 113,115,119. Discrepancies of Thomas' birthdates are due to approximations rather than actual dates which seldom were recorded for slave births,

91. Many former slaves chose the 25th of December, Jesus' birthday as they might explain, to be their birthday. On different documents both Thomas Patience and Crowder Patience's date of birth was recorded as Christmas day.
Moss. *Deeply Rooted*, Thomas on 113, Crowder's obituary on 51.

Chapter 14
Valuable Clue From North Carolina

92. Moss, *Deeply Rooted*, 91.

93. *23andMe* kits can be ordered online: https://www.23andMe.com/compare-dna-tests/
A sample of one's saliva is mailed to the company for analysis. Not only is one's ethnicity reported, but also a list of relatives who have taken the same test.

94. *23andMe* DNA report.

95. Every plant and animal species has a set number of chromosomes that appear in pairs, humans with 23 pairs. Joseph Lawrence Jr. and Juanita Patience Moss share four segments on the 10th chromosome.

For more information on the human genome, see National Human Genome Research Institute:
https://www.genome.gov/26524120/chromosomes-fact-sheet

Chapter 15
The 154-Year-Old-Mystery Is Solved

96. *Ancestry.com*. Federal Census for 1870.
97. *Ibid*, Federal Census for 1880.
98. *Ibid*, Federal Census for 1900.
99. *Ibid*, Federal Census for 1910.
100. *Ibid*, Federal Census for 1920.
101. Moss. *Deeply Rooted*, 125.

Chapter 16
Concluding Evidence

102. Also called fugitives and/or refugees. The term "contraband" was first introduced by Major General Benjamin Butler in 1861 at Fort Monroe, Virginia. He considered that since the absconding slaves were Confederate "property," then they were contraband or "spoils of war" and not to be returned to their owners. The term continued throughout the war to refer to the runaways. Contrabands were the "freedmen" on Roanoke Island where The Freedmen's Colony was formed by missionaries. After

the war ceased, The Freedman's Bureau was formed to aid former slaves.

103. A Chattel Mortgage is a loan that uses moveable personal property as collateral. Slaves were chattel prior to the Civil War.

104. Moss, *Deeply Rooted,* 84-85.

105.*The Andinka Dictionary.* "Sankofa is a constant reminder that past experience must be a guide for the future. Learn from or build on the past."

African American Civil War Museum
Entrance
1925 Vermont Avenue NW
Washington, D.C.

(photo by Reba N. Burruss-Barnes, Publicist)

2016

SOURCES

ARCHIVES

African American Civil War Museum, Washington, D.C.
Allen County Public Library, Fort Wayne, Indiana.
Anthracite Heritage Museum, Scranton, Pa.
Chowan County Courthouse, Edenton, N.C.
Chowan County, NC. Register of Deeds.
Dillsburg Historical Society, Dillsburg, Pa.
Fairfax County Public Library, Alexandria, Va.
Fairfax County Public Library, Fairfax, Va.
Fort Raleigh National Historic Site, Roanoke Island, N.C.
Gettysburg National Park, Gettysburg, Pa.
Kinston African American Civil War Museum, Kinston, N.C.
Library of Congress, Washington, D.C.
Living History Weekend, Plymouth, N.C.
Luzerne County Historical Society, Wilkes-Barre, Pa.
National Archives, Washington, D.C.
National Civil War Museum, Harrisburg, Pa.
National Museum of African American History and Culture, Washington, D.C.
North Carolina State Library and Archives, Raleigh, N.C.
North Carolina Museum of History, Raleigh, N.C.
North Carolina Estate files, 1663-1779,The Estate of Margaret L. Warren,1878.
Osterhout Public Library, Wilkes-Barre, Pa.
Outer Banks History Center, Roanoke Island, N.C.
Pennsylvania Veterans Burial Cards, 1777-1999.
Port O' Plymouth Museum, Plymouth, N.C.
Remembrance Day, Gettysburg, Pa.
Shepard-Pruden Public Library, Edenton, N.C.
Sherwood Library, Alexandria, Va.
War College at Carlisle Barracks, Harrisburg, Pa.
Washington County Historical Society, Plymouth, N.C.
West Pittston Historical Society, West Pittston, Pa.
West Pittston Public Library, West Pittston, Pa.
Wilkes University Library, Wilkes-Barre, Pa.

BOOKS

Ball, Edward. *Slaves in the Family*. New York: Farrar, Straus and Girox,1998.

Barrett, John Gilchrist. *North Carolina as a Civil War Battleground 1861-1865*. Raleigh: Division of Archives and History, N.C., Department of Cultural Resources. 7th printing, 1987.

Bates, Samuel P. *History of Pennsylvania Volunteers 1861-65*. Harrisburg, Pa.: B. Singerly, State Printer, Vol. 3, 1869-1871.

Bentley, George R. *A History of the Freedman's Bureau*. Philadelphia. Pa.: University of Pennsylvania, 1955.

Blockson, Charles L. *Black Genealogy*. Baltimore, Maryland: Black Classic Press, 1977.

Boyce, W. Scott. *Economics and Social History of Chowan County, North Carolina 1880-1915*, Vol. LXXXVI, no. 1. New York: Columbia University, 1917.

Burroughs, Tony. *Black Roots: A Beginner's Guide to Tracing the African American Family Tree*. New York: Simon and Schuster, 2001.

Byers, Paula. (ed.) *African-American Genealogical Sourcebook*. Detroit: Gale Research, 1995.

Caldwell, Arthur. (ed.) *History of the American Negro, North Carolina Edition* Vol. IV. Atlanta, Ga.: A. B. Caldwell Publishing Company, 1921.

Catton, Bruce. *The American Heritage: New History of the Civil War*. New York: Viking, 1960.

Cecelski, David S. *The Waterman's Song: Slavery and Freedom in Maritime North Carolina*. Chapel Hill, N.C.: The University of North Carolina Press, 2001.

Chaitin, Peter M. *The Civil War: The Coastal War*. Alexandria, Virginia: Time-Life Books, 1984.

Click, Patricia C. *Time Full of Trial: The Roanoke Island Freedmen's Colony 1862-1867*. Chapel Hill: University of North Carolina Press, 2001.

Cooper, Willie. *The Forgotten Legacy: The Black Soldiers and Sailors Who Fought in the Civil War 1862-1866.* Jamaica, N.Y.: Bravin Publishing, LLC, 2010.

Cornish, Dudley Taylor. *The Sable Arm: Negro Troops in the Union Army 1861-1865.* New York: W.W. Norton & Co., Inc., 1966.

Crabtree, Beth Gilbert and James Patton. (eds) *Journal of a Secesh Lady: The Diary of Catherine Ann Devereaux Edmondson 1860-1866.* Raleigh, N.C.: Division of Archives and History, 1979.

Davis, Burke. *The Civil War: Strange and Fascinating Facts.* New York: Crown Publishers, 1982.

Davis, Kenneth C. *Don't Know Much About the Civil War.* New York: Avon Books, 1966.

Dickey, Luther S. *History of the 103rd Regiment: Pennsylvania Veteran Voluntary Infantry 1861-1865.* Chicago, Illinois: L.S. Dickey, 1910.

Dyer, Frederick H. *A Compendium of the War of the Rebellion, Compiled and Arranged From Official Records of the Federal and Confederate Armies, Reports of the Adjutant Generals of the Several States, the Army Regiments, & Other Reliable Documents and Sources.* Des Moines: Dyer Publishing Co., 1908.

Elliot, Robert G. *Ironclad of the Roanoke: Gilbert Elliot's Albemarle.* Shippensburg, Pa.: White Mane Books, 1999.

Fears, Mary L. Jackson. *Slave Ancestral Research: It's Something Else.* Bowie, Md.: Heritage Books, 1995.

Fogel, Robert William and Stanley L. Engerman, *Time on the Cross: The Economics of American Negro Slavery.* Boston: Little, Brown and Company, 1974.

Foote, Shelby. *The Civil War. A Narrative: Red River to Appomattox.* New York: Random House, 1958.

Franklin, John Hope and Alfred A Moss. *From Slavery to Freedom: A History of African Americans,* 7th Edition. New York: McGraw-Hill, Inc., 1994.

Franklin, John Hope and Loren Schweninger. *Runaway Slaves: Rebels on the Plantation.* New York, N.Y.: Oxford University Press, 1999.

Gancus, Ronald. Research by Jack Blair and Dick Dugan. *The Hardluck Regiment: The Pennsylvania One Hundred and Third.* Butler, Pa.: Meching Bookbindery, 1998.

Garrison, Webb. *Civil War Curiosities: Strange Stories, Oddities, Events and Coincidences.* Nashville: Rutledge Hill Press, 1994.

Genovese, Eugene D. *Roll Jordan Roll: The World the Slaves Made.* New York: Vintage Books, A Division of Random House, 1973.

Gladstone, William A. *United States Colored Troops 1863-1867.* Gettysburg, Pa.: Thomas, 1990.

Glatthaar, Joseph T. *Forged in Battle: The Civil War Alliance of Black Soldiers and White Officers.* New York: The Free Press, 1990.

Goss, Sergeant Warren Lee. *The Soldier's Story of His Captivity at Andersonville, Bell Isle, and Other Rebel Prisons.* Boston: Lee and Shepard Publishers, 1866.

Green, Robert Ewell. *Black Defenders of America 1775-1973.* Chicago: Johnson Publishing Co., Inc., 1974.

Groene, Bertram H. *Tracing Your Civil War Ancestor.* Winston-Salem, N.C.: John F. Blair, 1995.

Guide to Genealogical Research in the National Archives of the United States, 3rd edition. National Archives and Records Administration, 2000.

Haskins, Jim. *Black, Blue & Gray: African Americans in the Civil War.* Simon & Schuster Books for Young Readers, 1998.

Hinds, John W. *Invasion and Conquest of North Carolina: Anatomy of a Gunboat War.* Shippensburg, Pa.: Beidel Printing House, Inc., 1923.

Hurmence, Belinda. *Before Freedom: When I Just Can Remember.* John F. Blair, Publisher, Winston-Salem, N.C., 1989.

_____, *My Folks Don't Want Me to Talk About Slavery: Twenty-one Histories of Former North Carolina Slaves.* Winston-Salem, N.C.: John F. Blair Publisher, 1994.

_____, *We Lived in a Little Cabin in the Yard.* Winston Salem, N.C.: John F. Blair, 1994.

Jacobs, Harriet A. *Incidents in the Life of a Slave Girl.* ed. by Ellen Fagan Yellin. Cambridge, Massachusetts: Harvard University Press, 1987.

Johnson, Charles and Patricia Smith and the WGBH Series Research Team. *Africans in America.* New York: Harcourt Brace & Company, 1998.

La Barre, Steven M. *The Fifth Massachusetts Colored Cavalry in the Civil War.* Jefferson, N.C.: McFarland & Co., Inc., 2016.

Mahood, Wayne. *The Plymouth Pilgrims: A History of the 85th New York Volunteer Infantry.* Hightstown, N.J.: Longstreet House, 1991.

_____, Editor. Charlie Mosher's Civil War: From Fair Oaks to Andersonville with the Plymouth Pilgrims (85th N.Y. Infantry). Hightstown, N.J.: Longstreet House, 1994.

McElroy, John. *Andersonville: A Story of Rebel Prisons.* Toledo: D. R. Locke, 1879.

McPherson, James M. *The Negro's Civil War: How American Negroes Felt and Acted During The War For The Union.* New York: Pantheon Books, 1965.

_____, *Battle Cry for Freedom: The Civil War Era.* New York: Oxford University Press, 1998.

Merrill, J. W. *Records of the 24th Independent Battery, N.Y. Light U.S.V.* Published for the Ladies' Cemetery Association of Perry, N.Y., 1870.

Moss, Emerson I. *African-Americans in the Wyoming Valley.* Wilkes-Barre, Pa.: Wyoming Historical and Geological Society and the Wilkes University Press, 1992.

Moss, Juanita Patience. *Anthracite Coal Art by Charles Edgar Patience.* Westminster, Md.: Heritage Books, 2006.

_____, *Battle of Plymouth, April 17-20, 1864: The Last Confederate Victory.* Bowie, Md.: Heritage Books, 2003.

_____, *Created to Be Free.* Bowie, Md.: Heritage Books, 2001.

_____, *Forgotten Black Soldiers Who Served in White Regiments During the Civil War.* Revised Vol. Berwyn Heights, Md.: Heritage Books, 2008.

_____, *Forgotten Black Soldiers Who Served in White Regiments During the Civil War.* Vol. II. Berwyn Heights, Md.: Heritage Books, 2014.

Mullane, Deirdre. (ed.) *Crossing the Danger Water: Three Hundred Years of African-American Writing.* New York: Anchor Books, Doubleday, 1993.

Nationals Park Service. "Freedom Comes to Roanoke Island: A Story of the Civil War," National Parks Service, Fort Raleigh National Historical Site, Roanoke Island, N.C.

Nevins, Allan. *The War For The Union,* Vol. II: *War Becomes Revolution.* New York: Charles Scribner and Sons, 1960.

Patterson, Christine. *The Black Experience in Wyoming Valley.* Wilkes-Barre, Pa.: Wilkes College Press, 1984.

Pictorial History of the Civil War in the United States of America. Philadelphia, Pa.: G. W. Childs, 1868.

Quarles, Benjamin. *The Negro in the Civil War.* A Da Capo Paperback, New York: A Subsidiary of Plenum Publishing Corp., 1953.

Redkey, Edwin S. *A Grand Army of Black Men.* Cambridge: Cambridge University Press, 1992.

Salvatore, Nick. *We All Got History: The Memory Books of Amos Webber.* New York: Times Books, 1996.

Spruill-Redford, Dorothy with Michael D'Orso. *Somerset Homecoming: Recovering a Lost Heritage.* Chapel Hill: The University of North Carolina Press, 1988.

Streets, David H. *Slave Genealogy: A Research Guide With Case Studies.* Bowie, Maryland: Heritage Books, 1986.

The Roster of Union Soldiers 1861-65. Wilmington, N.C.: Broadfoot Publishing Company, 1998.

The War of the Rebellion: A Compilation of the Official Records of the Union and Confederate Armies. 128 Volumes, Washington, D.C.: Government Printing Office, 1880-1891.

Thomas, Velma Maia. *Lest We Forget: The Passage From Africa to Slavery and Emancipation.* New York: Crown Publishers, 1997.

Trotter, William R. *Ironclads and Columbiads: The Civil War in North Carolina: The Coast.* Winston-Salem: John F. Blair, 1989.

Trudeau, Noah Andre. *Men of War: Black Troops in the Civil War 1862-1865.* Boston, Massachusetts: Little, Brown & Co., 1998.

Vlach, John Michael. *Back of the Big House: The Architecture of Plantation Slavery.* Chapel Hill, N.C.: The University of North Carolina Press, 1993.

War of the Rebellion. O.R. of Union and Confederate Armies. Series 2, Vol. 7. Published under the direction of the Hon. Russell A. Alger, Sec'y of War, Brig. Gen. Fred C. Ainsworth, Chief of the Record and Pension Office War Dept. and Jr. Joseph W. Kirkely, Washington, D.C.: Government Printing Office, 1899.

Ward, Geoffrey C. with Richard and Ken Burns. *The Civil War: An Illustrated History.* New York: Alfred A. Knopf, Inc., 1990.

Warner, John Dwight, Jr. *Crossed Sabres: A History of the Fifth Massachusetts Volunteer Cavalry, An African American Regiment in the Civil War.* A Dissertation, Boston College, The Graduate School of Arts and Sciences, May 1997.

Wesley, Charles H. *Negro Americans in the Civil War: From Slavery to Citizenship.* New York: Publishers Co., 1967.

Whitacre, Paula Tarnapol. *A Civil Life in an Uncivil Time, Julia Wilbur's Struggle for Purpose.* Potomac Books: University of Nebraska Press, 2017.

Williams, George Washington. *A History of the Negro Troops in the War of the Rebellion 1861-1865.* New York: Negro Universities Press, 1889.

Wilson, Joseph T., *The Black Phalanx: African American Soldiers in the War of Independence, the War of 1812 and the Civil War.* New York: Da Capo Press, 1994.

Woodtor, Dee Farmer. *Finding a Place Called Home: A Guide to African American Genealogy and Historical Identity.* New York: Random House, 1999.

NEWSPAPERS
Avon Life. May 2002.
Buffalo Morning Express. May 7, 1864.
Cincinnati Herald. October 31, 2013.
Cincinnati Inquirer, July 18, 2013.
Decatur Daily. November 18, 2008; July 9, 2009.
Harper's Weekly. November 19, 1864.
Hartford Courant. April 13, 1907; April 15, 1907.
Hartford Daily Times. September 3, 1907; October 15, 1907; April 20, 1908.
Living History Weekend. Supplement to the Roanoke Beacon. April 21, 2001; April 19-21, 2002.
Montclair Times, July 1983.
National Tribune Veterans Newspaper. May 1, 1864; August 1, 1889; September 19, 1889; January 9, 1902.
News and Observer. October 26, 1947.
Pittston Gazette. January 31, 1930; February 4, 1930.
Roanoke Beacon. August 1968; May 5, 1995; April 1998; April 18, 2001; April 17, 2002.
Smithfield Herald. March 18, 1924.
Sunday Independent. May 23, 1928.
Washington Post. July 17, 2008.

ARTICLES
"Ausbon House: One of Five to Pre-date Civil War." *The Roanoke Beacon Living History*, Plymouth, N.C., April 18, 2001, 8.

"Battle Scars Can Still Be Seen at Ausbon House." *The Roanoke Beacon Living History*, Plymouth, N.C., 1998, 4.

"Capture of Plymouth." *National Tribune Veterans Newspaper*, Library of Congress Newspaper Room, October 8, 1914.

"Confederate Forces Capture Plymouth, Battle of Plymouth-April 17-20. 1864." *The Roanoke Beacon,* Plymouth, N.C. (Filed at the Washington County Public Library, Plymouth, N.C.).

"Life and Death of the Ram 'Albemarle.'" *Historic Washington County,* Compiled and published by Washington County Historical Society, Plymouth, N.C.

"Mission Impossible" *Sea Classics*, Vol. 3, no. 4, July 1970, 14.

"North Carolina's Second Largest Battle." *The Roanoke Beacon Living History*, Plymouth, N.C., 1998, 4.

"Plymouth Again," *National Tribune Veteran's Newspaper*, Library of Congress Newspaper Room, September 19, 1889.

"Plymouth Last Major Victory For South in the War," *The Roanoke Beacon*, Plymouth, N.C., April 18, 2001, 6.

"Plymouth Pilgrims," *National Tribune Veteran's Newspaper*, Library of Congress Newspaper Room, May 1, 1864.

"Plymouth Pilgrims and How They Came to be Captured—A Survivor's Story," *National Tribune Veteran's Newspaper*, Library of Congress Newspaper Room, Washington, D.C.

"South Captures 2,500 Union Troops in Battle." *The Roanoke Beacon Living History*, April 18, 2001.

"The Capture of Plymouth," *Buffalo Morning Express*, May 1, 1864, 1. (Courtesy of B. Conrad Bush, historian of the 24th N.Y. Independent Battery Light Artillery).

"The Destruction of the 'Albemarle,'" *Harper's Weekly,* Vol. VIII, no. 412, New York, Saturday, November 19, 1864.

"The 1864 Siege of Plymouth, Civil War—A Good Time to Pray," *Roanoke Beacon*, Plymouth, N.C., August 6, 1986, 20. (Filed at Washington County Library, Plymouth, N.C.)

"The Fall of Plymouth 44 Years Ago To-Day," *The Hartford Daily Times,* Hartford, Conn., Monday, April 20, 1908. (Filed at Washington County Library, Plymouth, N.C.)

Black, Robert P. "Plymouth Pilgrims and How They Came to be Captured—A Survivor's Story." *Now and Then*, May 1, 1864.

Broadwell, J. H. "Ram Albemarle Sunk 110 Years Ago, Confederate's Personal Account of 1864 Battles." *Smithfield Herald*, March 18, 1924. (Filed at the Washington County Library, Plymouth, N.C.)

Brown, Jacob D. "Battle of Plymouth." *National Tribune Veterans Newspaper*, October 3, 1889.

Cimprich, John and Mainfort, Robert. "Fort Pillow Revisited: New Evidence About an Old Controversy." *Civil War History,* 1982, 293-306.

Dill, Lon. "Albemarle Scatters Fleet." *The Roanoke Beacon,* Plymouth, N.C., August 1968. (Filed at the Washington County Public Library, Plymouth, N.C.)

_____ "Confederate Ram Albemarle Scattered Whole Fleets But Lost to Tiny Launch." *The News and Observer,* Raleigh, N.C., Sunday morning, October 26, 1947, iv-3. (Filed at the Washington County Public Library, Plymouth, N.C.)

Gladstone, William A. "Black Integration in the Civil War: The Undercook." *Civil War News,* April 2008.

Jordan, Weymouth T., Jr. and Gerald W. Thomas. "Massacre at Plymouth: April 20, 1864." *North Carolina Historical Review* 72, April 1995.

Kammen, Carol. "African American Men in White New York Civil War Units." *New York History, Historical News and Views From The Empire State,* January 4, 2012.

McDaniel, Deangelo, "Black Union soldier to get marker almost 100 years after his death." *The Decatur Daily,* July 9, 2009.

_____ "Saving Decatur's History: Pastor, congressional aide want city to restore Sykes Cemetery." *The Decatur Daily,* November 18, 2008.

McPherson, James. "A War That Never Goes Away." *American Heritage,* March 1990, 41.

Nelson, Sharlene P. "The Battle of Plymouth Reported 106 Years Ago." (Filed at the Washington County Public Library, Plymouth, N.C.)

Pasher, Levi. "A History of Service," *The Leader Herald,* Gloversville, N.Y., 2013. (re: Medal of Honor recipient Pvt. Bruce Anderson).

Phelps, Shirley. "Ausbon House Dates Back to 1830's or 40's," *The Roanoke Beacon,* Plymouth, N.C.

Pierce, Annette. "Polishing a Historic Gem." *The Roanoke Beacon,* Plymouth, N.C., April 2001.

Schroeder, Cindy, "Cemeteries join in fight to mark veterans' graves," *The Cincinnati Enquirer*, July 18, 2013.

Slaybaugh, George H., "Battle of Plymouth," *National Tribune Veteran's Newspaper*, August 22, 1889.

_____ "How Cushing Destroyed the Albemarle," *National Tribune Veteran's Newspaper*, August 19, 1926.

Walker, Wyat Tee. *Somebody's Calling My Name: Black Sacred Music and Social Change.* Valley Forge, Pa.: Judson Press, 1979.

Wilson, Timothy. "African American: Honoring 'Great Men' of the Civil War," *Washington Post* Staff Writer, July 17, 2008, B06.

Yount, Dan, "Black, White Masons mark Black Civil War vets' graves," *The Cincinnati Herald*, October 31, 2013.

OTHER PUBLICATIONS

AAHGS News, Bi-monthly *Newsletter of the Afro-American Historical & Genealogical Society, Inc.*, May/June 1994.

First Annual Report, National Association, Relief of Destitute, Colored Woman and Children, McGill & Witherow, Printers and Stereotypers: Washington, D.C., 1864.

Washington County Genealogical Society Journal, August 1997.

ELECTRONIC

Ancestry.com

drbronsontours.com/pensionsunderstandingcivilwarpensions.html

Howard @HowardUniversity. Howard University Digital, Manuscript Division, 2015.

https://www.americancivilwarforum.com/blacksmith-during-the-acw-1944615.html

https://civilwartalk.com/threads/veterinary-medical-care-during-thecivil- war.130226/

https://cwemancipation.wordpress.com/2011/08/17/were-there-black-soldiers-in-july-1861-part-4/

http://cwppds.org/index.php/union-forces/103d-pa-infantry/roster/103d-pa-infantry-p/

https://en.wikipedia.org/wiki/

https://library.uncg.edu/slavery/petitions/history.nspx
http://thecincinnatiherald.com/news/2013/oct/31/black-white-masons-mark-black-civil-war-vets-grave/
httpps://mnaahc.si.ed/object/nmaahc_2016.70.2
http://users.aol.com/EvanSlaughrostp.html
https://www.arcchives.gov/education/lessons/blacks-civil-war
https://www.americancivilwarforum.com/blacksmith-during-the-acw-1944615.html
https://www.familysearch.org/wiki/en/United_States_Colored_Troops_in_the_Civil_War
https://www.familysearch.org/wiki/en/United_States_Civil_War_Pension_Record_(National_Institute)
https://www.genome.gov/26524120/chromosomes-fact-sheet
https://www.history.com/this-day-in-history/mason-and-dixon-draw-a-line
https://www.seniorliving.org/history/1890-civil-war-veterans-pension/
Regimental Roster of the 103rd Pennsylvania Infantry
rootsofedenton.org/blog-roots-of-edenton/july-10th-2014
The Art of a Confederate Prisoner at Point Lookout
www.1stalabamacavalryusv.com/roster/colored.aspx
www.newyorkhistoryblog.com/2012/01/african-american-men-in-white-ny-civil.html
www.sciencemadesimple.co.uk/curriculum-blogs/biology-blogs/what-is-dna
www.vistedenton.com/sites.php

This book has been written in the spirit of

 ***Sankofa*[105]**

"Go Back To Fetch It"

TESTIMONIALS

Re-enactor Michael Hinton, 23rd USCT

Historic Blenheim/Civil War Interpretive Center
Fairfax, VA
2015
(photo by Reba N. Burruss-Barnes)

"On behalf of all USCT's past and present. Your spirit, bravery and legacy will never be forgotten. We, your sons and daughters, at every opportunity will celebrate, educate and preserve your contribution to the fabric of this country."

Ruth L. Baskerville, Ph.D, Educator, Author, Ghostwriter:

"This 154-year-old mystery of lineage was a riveting book that kept me turning pages to the end. Dr. Moss was persistent, careful and deliberate in researching until she found the link between two of her ancestors. It inspired me to dig deeper into my ancestry. This is a 'must read' for sure!"

Reba N. Burruss-Barnes, Publicist / Photographer
CEO - REBAssociates Resource Network International

"It has been a blessing to do research with Dr. Moss for nearly twenty years. We have met people who had the next piece to her puzzle or given us first-hand directions to find details of her family history.

We have driven to and fro while singing 'Order My Steps, Lord' or 'Hush, Somebody's Calling My Name.' We found situations that were seemingly unrelated, yet each time a puzzle piece was added to her 'JOURNEY FROM THE PAST.'

Her ninth book, <u>Deeply Rooted in North Carolina</u> has been a dream and a well-stated goal for a long time. Now, the book has been published sharing the researched documents, previously published books and my photographs of her reaching back in time to solve the mystery of who Pvt. Thomas Patience might be to her great-grandfather Pvt. Crowder Patience.

Whether she and I were chatting about family and life goals or working hard on programs and research strategy, she has been a delight to challenge and encourage me.

Cheryl M. Chevalier, Ph.D, Educator, Author:

"In <u>Deeply Rooted in North Carolina</u>, Dr. Moss is historian, family griot, and teacher. As family griot she leads the reader in the discovery not only of her family roots but also in learning more of the role of absconding slaves in Civil War military history. As historian Dr. Moss provides in her Bibliography a plethora of archival resources for readers who would do their own research. As teacher she models how to think in questions and search for answers as readers begin their own journeys of discovery. As the Great-Granddaughter of a freeman who absconded from slavery, Dr. Moss demonstrates how families can discover their roots and for the descendants of slaves that is powerful."

Joseph R. Lawrence Jr., Lawrence family griot:

"I submitted my 23andme DNA kit, looking to add more names to my ancestry list. I didn't have any idea of what it would lead to. I found a branch of my family I didn't know existed. Finding that branch gave me the knowledge that my 3rd great grandfather fought in the Civil War. Seeing his name on the Wall of Honor at the African American Civil War Memorial gave me a unforgettable feeling of pride. The smile on my face was huge. Thank you, Cousin Juanita."

Christine Patterson, Patterson family griot:

"In 2002 I was in Washington, D.C. on a business trip and I asked Juanita if she would take me to the Civil War Monument to see my Great-grandfather Samuel Patterson's name inscribed on the Wall. After locating the 5th MA Cavalry and my great-grand father, Juanita spotted the name of Thomas Patience and was immediately intrigued. As fate would intervene, the following summer, Juanita came to teach in my Summer Bridge Program at Indiana University-Purdue University Fort Wayne, Indiana. It was a win-win for my students benefited from

her talents and Juanita benefited from the Allen County Public Library. At the time and I believe it still is the second largest genealogy archive in the nation. Juanita was in her element. I felt like Juanita was Sherlock and I was Watson, "Let the Chase begin." It has been a wonderful journey from the Civil War Monument where she first encountered the name of Thomas Patience to the place of his birth. The need for truth will lead us into unexpected places beyond our imagination."

Carolyn Corpening Collins Rowe, Former President, Afro-American Historical and Genealogical Society, Inc.:

"Juanita Patience Moss is a story teller extraordinaire. She uses her considerable skills as a researcher and writer to bring history and genealogy together to form very compelling narratives. In the process of documenting her great grandfather's military service during the Civil War, she uncovered a little-known piece of American history. She discovered that her great grandfather, Crowder Paciens/Patience, was not among the ranks of the U.S. Colored Troops, but was instead a soldier in a White regiment. 'No way', 'not possible', 'no such thing', said most historians and academics at the time. Dr. Moss, confident in her family's oral history and armed with her great grandfather's military papers, not only proved that his service was indeed in a white regiment, but found many other African-American men who had served in white regiments. She shared this information in the book <u>Forgotten Black Soldiers Who Served in White Regiments During the Civil War</u>. Following a recent revelation in a DNA report, she has written a book entitled <u>Deeply Rooted in North Carolina</u> about finding a long-lost branch of her family. This book, like <u>Forgotten Black Soldiers,</u> will be an interesting and informative combination of genealogy and history."

Earl L. Ijames, Historian, Curator of North Carolina Museum of History, Raleigh, N.C.

"Re: Thomas Patience and African American Ancestry with French Lineage

I have had the privilege to work with many genealogists, historians, and academics, among others, throughout my career. Dr. Juanita Patience Moss and her continuing research in American history has been a refreshing experience that has allowed us to delve into lesser known aspects of our culture and history. Dr. Moss' work has also helped me as a historian better explain the evolution of our nation to burgeoning historians and lay people about colonial and antebellum settlement of what is known today as North Carolina.

Dr. J, as she is known in the academic world, introduced herself to me while researching at the North Carolina State Archives during the 2005 United States Colored Troops Symposium. I worked as an Archivist at that time. Dr. J's research request included a question that I wondered why more Americans did not ask. That is- "Were there French slave holders?"

As a 7th generation North Carolinian by the "Ijames" surname I have some familiarity with French, Huguenot and African migration to America, North Carolina, in particular. With an academic knowledge of Francophone slavery and a mastery of primary sources I was able to assist Dr. J by helping to better understand how the French nomenclature became Anglicized with a northeastern North Carolina southern dialect during the antebellum era. Dr. Moss' perfect English pronunciation of "Brahal Road" near Edenton, North Carolina immediately triggered my antennae since "Brahal" is not, nor has been a documented surname in Chowan County or any county in the vicinity. When Dr. Moss produced further evidence a slaveholder named "Bre- - - -" in her lineage I suggested she drive "down east" to get a lay of the land and hear locals speak.

    Before heading to the colonial mecca of North Carolina I consulted more with Dr. Moss about the impact The Haitian Revolution had upon coastal Carolina, especially northeastern North Carolina. Many French slaveholders fled Gen. Toussaint L' Overture and the largest standing army in the western hemisphere between 1791 and 1804 for laws and customs more aligned with their sugar plantations in the West Indies. Therefore, places like Savannah, GA; Charleston, SC and Edenton, NC became refuges for French planters. I also recommended that she research the North Carolina Session Laws that could possibly reflect their arrival. Surely, Dr. J followed advice to the letter and located a 1795 law requiring French planters to register upon arrival in the State of North Carolina. In those records, Dr. Moss located a Francophone planter from Guadeloupe named Francios Breole(s).

    Which brings us back to Thomas Patience and the original question. Dr. J and I agreed that "Patience" is likely a French name and that it could have been easily Anglicized by the 20th century since it has the same spelling "en Anglais". As one last assignment to Dr. Moss, I suggested that Thomas Patience (b. 1835) may have survived long enough to have a North Carolina Death Certificate. The state began recording vital records statewide in October 1913. Thomas Patience could have survived into his eighties to have been recorded by the State Health Department and Chowan County Register of Deeds.

    One of the greatest joys of my career was when Dr. Moss emerged from the microfilm room with a wide smile, a hug for my neck and a 1929 Death Certificate of Thomas Patience, aged 93! Dr. J had successfully operated on locating a Civil War era ancestor while stringing together some historical pearls along the way."

December 2018

AUTHOR

(photo by Reba N. Burruss-Barnes, Publicist)

JUANITA PATIENCE MOSS, family griot, educator, author, and presenter, is the daughter of the late Cora and Charles Edgar Patience, renowned anthracite coal sculptor from northeastern Pennsylvania. After graduating from the West Pittston High School, she attended Bennett College in Greensboro, N. C., Alma Mater of her step-mother Alice Patterson Patience. Afterwards she completed her B.S. degree at Wilkes College, Wilkes-Barre, Penna.; earned a M.A. degree at Fairleigh Dickinson University, Rutherford, N.J.; and received an Honorary Doctor of Humanities from King's College, Wilkes-Barre, Penna.

After teaching high school biology for thirty-three years at Bloomfield High School, Bloomfield, N.J., she re-located to Alexandria, Virginia. Soon afterwards she would develop interests in genealogy and history, resulting in the publication of nine books.

OTHER PUBLICATIONS
BY
Dr. JUANITA PATIENCE MOSS
www.journeyfromthepast.com

Anthracite Coal Art by Charles Edgar Patience

Created to Be Free

Battle of Plymouth, N.C., April 17-20, 1864: The Last Confederate Victory

Forgotten Black Soldiers Who Served in White Regiments During the Civil War Vols. I & II

Tell Me Why Dear Bennett: Memoirs of Bennett College Belles, Vols. I, II, & III.

Journey From the Past
www.journeyfromthepast.com

www.ingramcontent.com/pod-product-compliance
Lightning Source LLC
Chambersburg PA
CBHW070917180426
43192CB00037B/1673